SELF AS

HOW TO

TAX RETURN

SELF ASSESSMENT
HOW TO FILL IN YOUR TAX RETURN

STEP-BY-STEP ADVICE FOR THE 1998 TAX RETURN

More than 125 tax tips

Niki Chesworth

Published in
association with

THE INSTITUTE OF CHARTERED ACCOUNTANTS IN ENGLAND & WALES

KOGAN PAGE

First published in 1997
Second edition 1998

Kogan Page Limited
120 Pentonville Road
London N1 9JN

British Library Cataloguing in Publication Data

A CIP record for this book is available from the British Library.

ISBN 0 7494 2653 5

Typeset by Saxon Graphics Ltd, Derby
Printed and bound in Great Britain by Clays Ltd, St Ives plc

CONTENTS

Dates to Remember *vi*

Acknowledgements *vii*

Introduction *viii*

Part 1: What You Need to Know

1. *A Guide to Self Assessment* 3
2. *A Guide to Filling in Your Tax Return* 7
3. *A Beginner's Guide to Income Tax* 11
4. *Tips on Filling in Your Tax Return* 23

Part 2: Step-by-Step Guide to Filling in the Main Tax Return

5. *The Questionnaire* 27
6. *Savings Interest and Share Dividends* 36
7. *Pensions, Social Security Benefits, Maintenance Payments and Other Income* 45
8. *Tax Relief on Pensions, Mortgages, Charitable Giving and Other Loans and Investments* 61
9. *Tax Allowances* 81

Part 3: Employment

10. *Employer's Details and Pay* 97
11. *Employee Benefits and Expenses* 103
12. *Redundancy, Lump-Sum and Compensation Payments* 121
13. *Allowable Employee Expenses* 125

Part 4: A Guide to Filling in the Other Supplementary Pages

14. *Share Schemes* 133
15. *Self-Employment* 139
16. *Partnerships* 155
17. *Land and Property* 157

18. Foreign Income *164*
19. Trusts *170*
20. Capital Gains *174*
21. Non-Residence *183*

Part 5: A Step-by-Step Guide to Filling in the Rest of Your Main Tax Return
22. The Remaining Questions *189*

Appendix 1: Calculating Your Own Tax *195*

Index *203*

DATES TO REMEMBER

When	Who	What
By 31 January 1998	Everyone who was sent a 1996/97 Tax Return	Had to complete it and send it back and pay their tax bill for the 1996/97 tax year
6 April 1998	Everyone who receives a Tax Return	Will be sent a Tax Return for the 1997/98 year
By 31 May 1998	Employees	Should be given their P60 for the 1997/98 tax year by their employer detailing their salary, Income Tax and National Insurance
By 6 July 1999	Employees with expenses and other benefits such as company cars	Will get details of these from their employer for the 1997/98 tax year on form P11D or P9D
By 31st July 1999	People paying tax 'on account' – mainly the self-employed	Should pay their second tax instalment for the 1997/98 tax year. You will receive a demand if this affects you
By 30 September 1998	People who *do not* want to calculate their own tax bill. PAYE employees who want the tax they owe collected through their PAYE code (up to £1000)	Should send back their completed Tax Return
By 5 October 1998	People with new sources of income in the 1997/98 tax year	Should inform the Inland Revenue so they can be sent any additional pages they need to complete their Tax Return
By 31 January 1999	Everyone who receives a Tax Return	Should send it back by now and pay any tax due
1 February 1999	Anyone who had not sent their Tax Return back by yesterday's deadline	Gets fined £100
28 February 1999	Anyone still owing tax due on 31 January 1999	Suffers a 5 per cent surcharge on the tax they owe
Before 31 January 2000	Everyone can still hear from the Inland Revenue about their 1997/98 Tax Return	Because if the Inland Revenue has any queries they will contact you within 12 months

Tax is a very technical and complex subject and some tax rules are open to interpretation. That is why there is a whole army of accountants employed to make the most of the rules and challenge them. Every effort has been made to ensure the accuracy of this book. Technical tax points have been checked with the Inland Revenue and several qualified accountants. However, as tax rules are open to interpretation – and in some cases negotiation with your tax inspector – and the advice you receive can vary from Tax Office to Tax Office, if you are unsure about any point, ask your tax inspector. The number of your Tax Office is written on the top of your Tax Return.

Acknowledgements

I would like to thank all those who have helped me to produce this book, particularly: my publishers Kogan Page; the Inland Revenue press office (who have been most helpful); accountants who have given me help and advice including Joseph Robinson and Wendy Tresise; and the non-tax experts – particularly Guy Kendall – who have ruthlessly read the manuscript to ensure that those with little or no knowledge of tax should be able understand what I have written and act on the advice.

INTRODUCTION

WHO SHOULD READ THIS BOOK

Almost nine million taxpayers are sent a Tax Return every April. Most of these should be able to fill in their Tax Return without seeking help from a professional adviser. However, some taxpayers with more complicated financial affairs may benefit from employing an accountant.

This book is aimed at those who:

- ❑ don't need – or want – to pay someone else to fill in their Tax Return;
- ❑ want to employ a professional tax adviser but also want to know how the tax system works, what information they need to give their adviser and ways to save tax.
- ❑ want to save tax – the Inland Revenue estimates some six million people are owed £500 million in tax refunds alone.

Those who will benefit from reading this book include:

Higher-rate taxpayers

- ❑ Who want to know how to reduce the amount of higher-rate tax they pay.
- ❑ Who want to claim maximum tax relief.

Those with employee perks

- ❑ Who want to know how they can save tax on their employee benefits such as company cars.
- ❑ Who want to understand how these benefits are taxed.
- ❑ Who want to calculate if they should swap benefits for extra pay.

Those with additional freelance earnings

- ❑ Who want to understand how these are taxed.
- ❑ Who want to know how they can reduce the tax they must pay.

The self-employed

- ❑ Who opt to prepare their own accounts.
- ❑ Who want to know what they can claim as expenses to reduce their tax bill.

Anyone with savings and investments

- ❑ Who wants to know what they must declare to the Inland Revenue.
- ❑ Who wants to make the most of tax breaks.

Property owners

- ❑ Who let – or plan to let – all or part of their main home.
- ❑ Who want to know how they will be taxed on their second/holiday home.

Anyone who is married, divorced or has children

- ❑ Who needs to know what tax allowances they can claim.
- ❑ Who wants to know how marriage and divorce will affect their tax situation.
- ❑ Who wants know how they can save tax on maintenance payments.

Anyone in receipt of a pension

- ❑ Who needs to calculate how their income will affect their tax allowances.
- ❑ Who wants to structure their finances so they pay less tax.

THE AIMS OF THIS BOOK

1. To help you fill in your Tax Return using a step-by-step guide.
2. To help you save tax.

3. To translate complex tax terms into plain English.
4. To explain how the tax system works.
5. To take the fear out of tax.
6. To remind you of what you must do and by when.
7. To show you how to organize your finances to reduce your future tax bills.
8. To tell you how to avoid Inland Revenue fines and investigations.
9. To show you where you can get further help and advice.
10. To be value for money . . . **you should save far more than the cost of this book.**

Note: This book is aimed at employees, those with savings and investments and those who have small amounts of self-employed or freelance earnings. Kogan Page publishes a separate book for the self-employed called *Self Assessment for the Small Business and Self-Employed.* The self-employed with a turnover in excess of £15,000 will find that book more suitable.

PART
1

WHAT YOU NEED TO KNOW

1

A GUIDE TO SELF ASSESSMENT

The first Self Assessment Tax Returns were sent out in April 1997, so you will probably already know what they look like and how much information you need to provide.

Tax Returns are issued by the Inland Revenue to ensure you pay the correct amount of Income Tax and Capital Gains Tax. However, in most cases there is very little extra tax to pay as most taxpayers already pay tax on much of their income. Tax is deducted automatically from employees' salaries, and banks, building societies and quoted companies also deduct tax from savings, investments and share dividends.

As a result most readers of this book will *only have to fill in 22 boxes of information on their Tax Return*. And much of this information is easy to supply as figures can simply be copied from other forms – without calculations.

WHAT SELF ASSESSMENT ALLOWS YOU TO DO

You can calculate your own tax if you want to

In theory Self Assessment means you must assess or calculate your own tax bill. But you may be relieved to know that in practice you **don't** actually have to do the calculations yourself – although you can if you want to. The Inland Revenue will calculate your tax bill, but you must send in your completed Tax Return promptly by **30 September 1998.**

WHAT SELF ASSESSMENT REQUIRES YOU TO DO

Complete your tax return on time

If you are/were sent a Tax Return covering the April 1997 to April 1998 tax year, you **must** complete it and return it by one of these two dates:

30 September 1998 if you want the Inland Revenue to calculate how much tax you owe ***or*** if you owe less than £1000 in tax and want that tax collected through your pay packet under the PAYE (Pay-As-You-Earn) tax system instead of paying a tax bill.

31 January 1999 all Tax Returns must be submitted by this date.

. . . or you will be fined

The fixed penalty for Tax Returns not sent back by 31 January is **£100**. If your Return is still outstanding six months later you will be fined a further **£100.** However, if you owe £100 or less in outstanding tax, the penalty will be reduced to the amount of tax owed.

These fixed fines are charged automatically.

If the Inland Revenue thinks that charging you the fixed penalty is not going to make you send back your Tax Return, fines of up to **£60 a day** can be levied.

> **Warning:** If you do not send back your Tax Return and pay your tax by the 31 January 1999 deadline, the Inland Revenue may bill you for what it thinks you owe, plus penalties and surcharges, and collect that amount.

Pay any outstanding tax on time

All tax due for the 1997/98 tax year must be paid by **31 January 1999** at the very latest. If you pay tax *on account* – by instalments – you will also have to make two interim tax payments. The first of these was due on 31 January 1998 and the second is due on 31 July 1998. You will generally only be required to make these payments *on account* if you are self-employed, earn income from land and property or have large amounts of untaxed investment income.

If you owe a small amount of tax (less than £1000) and are an employee paid under PAYE, you may not get a tax bill at all provided you send in your Tax Return by 30 September 1998. The extra tax can be collected with the rest of your Income Tax from your pay.

If the Inland Revenue is calculating your tax bill you will be sent a tax demand before the 31 January 1999 deadline. If you – or your accountant – is calculating your tax bill you must pay the amount you think you owe.

. . . or you will be charged interest

You will be charged interest of 9.5 per cent (this rate is subject to change in line with base interest rates) on late payment of tax or if you pay too little tax. Note the rates are designed to give the Inland Revenue a commercial rate of return.

Any outstanding tax for the tax year ending April 1998 which is still unpaid as of 28 February 1999 will cost you an extra 5 per cent of the outstanding amount. So you will be surcharged for being only one month late. If you still have not paid your tax bill by 31 July 1999 the surcharge rises to 10 per cent.

Tell the Inland Revenue if you have any new sources of income

If you start to receive any untaxed income – for instance from freelance earnings or from letting out a property – you must tell the Inland Revenue within six months of the end of the tax year. So if you started to receive additional income in the 1997/98 tax year, the deadline is **5 October 1998.** If you do not inform the Inland Revenue, it cannot send you the necessary extra pages that make up your Tax Return. As such, your Tax Return could be incomplete or there may be a delay in sending it out. As a result you could face a fine or be charged interest on late payment of tax.

You must ask for a tax return if you need one but have not been sent one

Almost nine million Tax Returns are sent out by the Inland Revenue every April. But in some cases the Inland Revenue may not know that you need to fill one in. It is your responsibility to ask for one if you need to declare any additional income – it is not the Inland Revenue's responsibility to send you a Tax Return.

You must keep records

Self Assessment requires that you keep records of all income, expenses, assets and any other financial documents. This has been a requirement since April 1996, so if you haven't been keeping records – start **now.**

You must keep all documents for **at least 22 months** after the end of the tax year to which they relate. So for the April 1997 to April 1998 tax year you must keep records until February 2000.

However, if you are self-employed or a partner you must keep your tax records for **five years** after the date you send back your Tax Return.

Record keeping means looking after all financial documents from the Inland Revenue, your bank or building society and your employer, and keeping any paperwork relating to other sources of income and investments and the purchase or sale of assets that you may sell at a profit. You must set up a record-keeping system, keep documents safe and for as long as required and update your records regularly.

. . . or risk being fined

If you fail to keep adequate records to support information given on your Tax Return, the Inland Revenue may fine you up to £3000. Even if you do not get fined, failure to keep records will have other implications – you will find it much harder to fill in your Tax Return.

2

A GUIDE TO FILLING IN YOUR TAX RETURN

If you are sent a Tax Return you **must** fill it in and return it on time.

Tax Returns are sent out by the Inland Revenue every April to almost nine million taxpayers who need to declare additional income or profits or who need to claim tax relief or tax allowances, and to those who may need to pay additional tax on income that has been taxed at a lower rate. Your Tax Return is tailored to your individual circumstances. The information you give on your Tax Return is used to assess the amount of income tax and capital gains tax you owe, as well as National Insurance if you are self-employed or in partnership.

SHOULD I EMPLOY SOMEONE TO FILL IN MY TAX RETURN?

Half the work involved in filling in your Tax Return is in the preparation – getting the right documents and information. And as you will probably only have to fill in around 22 boxes you should be able to do this yourself. But you can employ an accountant or other tax adviser to fill in your Tax Return. Remember, you will still have to do a lot of the work yourself, collecting the relevant records and paperwork, and will have to know what information to give your accountant. However, employing an accountant is highly advisable if you have complicated tax affairs.

WHAT INFORMATION WILL I NEED?

You will need to have all your financial documents and statements to hand before you start to fill in your Tax Return. The exact paperwork you will require is listed in the step-by-step guide later in this book. However, this list covers most of the documents you will need:

- ❑ any documents given to you by your employer detailing pay, tax deducted and your employee benefits;
- ❑ all bank and building society passbooks and statements;
- ❑ details of any state benefits you have received;
- ❑ annual statements and details of any investments, shares and personal pensions;
- ❑ records of additional income – such as freelance earnings or income from rents – and any expenses incurred in earning this income;
- ❑ your accounts – including invoices, receipts, records of payments and expenses – if you are self-employed;
- ❑ details of any maintenance paid/received;
- ❑ any other financial documents.

WHAT IF I HAVEN'T GOT ALL THE FACTS AND FIGURES I NEED?

The information you require – and where to find this – is listed later in this book. But if, for some reason, the documents are not available or you cannot get an accurate figure, you can enter your best estimate. You must clearly mark it as an estimate and once you have obtained the accurate figure you must tell the Inland Revenue.

WHAT IF I MAKE A MISTAKE ON MY TAX RETURN?

When you send back your Tax Return the Inland Revenue will check it for obvious mistakes – for instance, you forgot to sign it or did not include the correct paperwork.

The Self Assessment rules allow for human error. *You can amend your Tax Return and tax assessment provided you do this within 12 months of the date you sent it back.* In most cases you will not be charged a penalty. However, you may be charged interest on tax you should have paid earlier.

HOW WILL THE INLAND REVENUE CHECK I AM PAYING THE RIGHT AMOUNT OF TAX?

The Inland Revenue performs spot checks on a small percentage of Tax Returns to make sure that taxpayers are not abusing Self Assessment to pay less tax.

Every Tax Return will be input into a computer and the calculations checked. So, even if you have calculated your own tax bill, the Tax Office will double check the figures. While the Tax Returns are being input into the computer, tax inspectors will use what is called their 'nose' – their instinct for spotting errors and those trying to evade tax.

If you have calculated the tax you owe yourself and you have made a mistake, the Inland Revenue will send you an amended calculation if necessary. If you disagree with any correction made, you can challenge it.

If the Inland Revenue decides it wants to investigate your tax affairs it will do so within 12 months of the date you sent in your Tax Return. That is why it is essential to keep records. An investigation can range from a straightforward question about how you have added up your figures to a full investigation. If you are selected for an enquiry you will be sent information telling you what to expect.

HOW CAN THE INLAND REVENUE HELP ME?

Most people are frightened of talking to the Inland Revenue for fear that they may find tax inspectors examining their financial affairs. However, you may be surprised to find out how helpful the Inland Revenue can be. And all advice and leaflets are free.

If you want help, advice or an information leaflet, ring the Inland Revenue at your Tax Office – the telephone number is printed on the top of your Tax Return. Or you can telephone your local Tax Enquiry Centre – the number is in the phone book. Switchboards are open to the public from 9am to 4.30pm and most offices are open for you to visit for at least eight hours a day. If you are embarrassed about asking a simple question, don't worry – Tax Office staff are used to dealing with all levels of enquiries.

You can also call the special Helpline set up by the Inland Revenue to deal with self-assessment enquiries, on 0645 000 444. The Helpline offers general advice on tax, is open in the evenings and at weekends and calls are charged at local rates.

Remember: If you write to the Inland Revenue, quote your tax reference number – it is printed on your Notice of Income Tax Coding, Statement of Account and on your Tax Return.

CAN I USE A COMPUTER TO HELP ME FILL IN MY TAX RETURN?

Yes. There are several software packages available to help you fill in your Tax Return and calculate your tax bill. However, they may not be Inland Revenue approved. If there is an error on your Tax Return you cannot use your computer as an excuse.

The Inland Revenue has its own computer package. It only covers the basic eight-page Tax Return and the extra pages covering employment.

For the moment, only accountants and other approved tax agents can send in completed Tax Returns electronically.

3

A BEGINNER'S GUIDE TO INCOME TAX

This chapter will help you to understand:

- why you are filling in certain boxes on your Tax Return;
- how the figures are worked out;
- which items and figures you do **not** have to include on your Tax Return.

As a result you should be able to:

- work out ways to cut your tax bill;
- organize your finances so you pay less tax in future;
- claim the maximum amount of tax allowances and tax relief.

This chapter looks at Income Tax because this is the main tax covered by your Tax Return. **Capital Gains Tax**, the tax on profits from the sale of shares, investments, second homes and other assets is covered later in the book in Chapter 20. The other 'tax' assessed using the Tax Return is **National Insurance if you are self-employed.** Details of the rates for the self-employed are included in Chapter 15 on self-employment.

This book looks at the rates in the tax year 6 April 1997 to 5 April 1998 – the year covered by the Tax Return sent out in April 1998.

TAX-FREE INCOME

Some types of income are tax free and **you do not have to include these on your Tax Return**. This includes:

- ❑ income from National Savings Certificates;
- ❑ the first £70 of interest from National Savings Bank ordinary accounts;
- ❑ premium bond prizes;
- ❑ proceeds from most life insurance policies;
- ❑ Save As You Earn bonuses;
- ❑ profit-related pay up to a maximum of £4000, reducing to £2000 between 1 January 1998 and 31 December 1998 or 20 per cent of your pay if this is lower (although this will be reduced to £1000 on 1 January 1999 and will then be phased out from 1 January 2000);
- ❑ income from Personal Equity Plans (PEPs) – however, these will be replaced from April 1999 by the new Individual Savings Account;
- ❑ redundancy pay (up to £30,000) and certain other payments when you lose a job;
- ❑ shares allocated to you by your employer under an approved profit-sharing scheme;
- ❑ local authority home improvement grants;
- ❑ most educational grants and scholarships;
- ❑ maintenance payments paid by your former spouse or the father of your children up to set limits and subject to certain conditions;
- ❑ some employee benefits such as a subsidized canteen (see Chapter 11 on employee benefits and expenses for more details);
- ❑ some social security benefits including:
  - child benefit and allowances;
  - housing benefits;
  - maternity allowance;
  - sickness benefit;
  - family credit;
  - income support (in most cases);
  - wounds or disability pensions;
  - war widow's pension;
  - disability living allowance;
  - widow's payment;
  - job release allowance to men aged 64 and over or women aged 59 and over;
  - attendance allowance;
  - severe disablement allowance;
  - Christmas bonus for pensioners;
  - industrial injury benefits.

Note: The Government plans to integrate the tax and benefits systems so the tax situation of certain benefits could change.

And the following do not count as income and so are not taxed:

- prizes and betting winnings including the lottery, competitions and gambling;
- gifts and presents (but not if they are for work done).

Note: If you sell something, this does not count as income but may be liable for Capital Gains Tax – the tax you pay on the profit you make when you sell an asset such as shares, investments, second homes and businesses (but not personal possessions).

If you inherit money or assets, these do not count as income either and as such are not taxed. However, if interest was earned on the estate (the amount of wealth and assets left by someone when they die) while that estate was being administered, you may have to pay tax on that income.

INCOME TAX RATES AND TAX BANDS

Income tax for the 1997/8 tax year was charged at three different *tax rates* on income that falls into different *tax bands*. You only pay each rate of income tax on income that falls within a tax band of earnings. This means that you can pay tax at the lower rate, basic rate and higher rate if you have income in each of these tax bands.

The amount of tax charged on each tax band has been calculated for you – see Table 3.1.

Table 3.1 *Income Tax: the different tax rates and tax bands*

Tax rate	%	Income Tax band Tax year 1997/98	Tax you will have to pay
Lower	20%	The first **£4100** of taxable income in excess of your allowances	(20% of £4100) **£820**
Basic	23%	The next **£4101** to **£26,100** of taxable income (£22,000 of income)	(23% of £22,000) **£5060**
Higher	40%	Taxable income in excess of **£26,100**	40% of income above this limit

These income bands are in addition to your tax allowance – so you only pay tax on income above your allowance. The income covered by your allowance is tax-free regardless of your rate of tax.

TAX ALLOWANCES

You don't have to pay tax on all of your income, profits or wealth. You are entitled to what is called a *tax allowance* – the amount you can earn **before** you have to pay tax.

The main allowances you will receive automatically or can claim are:

⇒ **Personal allowance.** Everyone has a personal allowance – but you are only allowed one. If you have more than one job or are an employee and self-employed, you can only set the personal allowance against one lot of income – usually your main source of income.

⇒ **Married couple's allowance.** This is in addition to your personal allowance and is given if you are married. If you wed part way through the tax year your allowance will be reduced proportionately. The allowance is given to the husband. The wife can claim half without her husband's consent and all of it with his agreement.

⇒ **Age allowances.** The personal allowance rises with age. To qualify for an age allowance you must have reached either 65 or 75 by the end of the tax year, 5 April 1998. The married couple's age allowance is also increased if either of the couple is aged 65 or over at the end of the tax year.

⇒ **Single parent allowance.** This is officially called the 'additional personal allowance'. It is given to those who have a child living with them who are single, separated, divorced or widowed.

How allowances reduce your tax bill

Your tax allowance is how much you can earn **before** paying tax, **not** the amount of tax you save. How much tax you save depends on your top rate of tax.

The personal tax allowance means that you do not have to pay tax on £4045 of taxable income in the April 1997 to April 1998 tax year. So the allowance reduces the amount of income that falls into the higher route tax bands.

If you would normally pay 23 per cent tax on that income, you save:

23% of £4045 = **£930**

However, if you are a higher rate taxpayer and pay 40 per cent tax on your highest earnings, your savings will be as follows:

40% of £4045 = **£1618**

But you can only save 40 per cent tax on income taxed at 40 per cent. So, if – before the allowance – only £1,000 of earnings would have fallen in the higher-rate tax bracket, you will only save 40 per cent on the £1000. Your savings on the remaining allowance of £3045 will be at the basic tax rate of 23 per cent.

Some allowances have *relief restrictions*, which means that the rate of tax relief is restricted to a certain rate of tax as in the case of the *married couple's allowance*. This means that instead of saving up to 40 per cent of the allowance you can only save 15 per cent.

So the tax savings are as follows for **both** basic-rate and higher-rate taxpayers:

15% of £1830 = **£275**

Special rules for pensioners

The age allowance given to those aged 65 and over has an *earnings restriction*. This means that if you had a total taxable income of more than £15,600 in the April 1997 to April 1998 tax year your allowances would be reduced by £1 for every £2 you earned over this limit. The allowance only stops being reduced when it is cut to the basic personal allowance of £4045. So the more you earn the less tax savings you make. This works as follows:

Pensioner A is 67 and has a total income from pensions and investments in the 1997/98 tax year of **£19,000.**

His age increased personal allowance (because he is over 65) is **£5220.**

But he can only earn **£15,600** before this allowance is reduced by £1 for every £2 he earns above this limit. So his allowance will be reduced as follows:

£19,000 (his income) – **£15,600** (the restriction) = **£3400**

So he earns £3400 more than the restriction.

The allowance is reduced by £1 for every £2 of earnings over the restriction. So:

£3400 divided by 2 = **£1700**:

So his allowance will be reduced by £1700:

£5220 (his age allowance) – **£1700** (the reduction as a result of the earnings restriction) = **£3520**

However, this is below the basic personal allowance of £4045, so his basic personal allowance will be **£4045**.

So he still has not used up £4045 – £3520 = **£525** of the reduction.

If you are married and do not use up the earnings reduction on your personal age allowance, the extra reduction is taken away from your married couple's allowance but again, it cannot be reduced to below the basic married. If you are not married, no further reduction is made. However, in Pensioner A's case his married couple's allowance will be reduced by £525. For a full listing of tax allowances and the resultant tax savings, see Table 3.2.

TAX CODES

Tax Codes are given to those who receive income under PAYE (Pay-As-You-Earn), the system for collecting taxes from wages and salaries and company pensions. The code adjusts your *tax allowances* so a greater or lesser amount of tax can be deducted from your salary or company pension before it is paid to you. This enables the Inland Revenue to collect any extra tax or give you additional tax relief. **Your Tax Code is your responsibility and it is up to you to check that your Code is correct**.

You may be sent a PAYE Coding Notice by the Inland Revenue every year or when your circumstances change. This will tell you what the Code is. You may also be able to find your Tax Code on your wage slip or your P45 (if you have lost your job or are moving jobs).

Table 3.2 *Tax allowances for the April 1997 – April 1998 tax year*

Type of allowance	1997/98 allowance	Amount of tax saving for basic rate taxpayer and rate at which tax savings are made	Amount of tax saving for higher rate taxpayer and rate at which tax savings are made
Standard personal allowance	£4045	£930 (at 23%)	£1618 (at 40%)
Standard married couple's allowance*	£1830	£275 (at 15%)	£275 (at 15%)
Aged 65 to 74: personal allowance	£5220	£1201 (at 23%)	£2088 (at 40%)
Aged 65 to 74: married couple's allowance*	£3185	£733 (at 15%)	£733 (at 15%)
Aged 75 and over personal allowance	£5400	£1242 (at 23%)	£2160 (at 40%)
Aged 75 and over married couple's allowance*	£3225	£484 (at 15%)	£484 (at 15%)
Additional personal allowance for single parents*	£1830	£275 (at 15%)	£275 (at 15%)
Widow's bereavement allowance*	£1830	£275 (at 15%)	£275 (at 15%)
Blind person allowance	£1280	£294 (at 23%)	£512 (at 40%)
Income limit for age-related allowances**	£15,600		

Notes

* Relief restricted to 15 per cent – this means that regardless of the tax rate you pay you can only get a tax saving at 15 per cent. This is to restrict the tax advantage and to make it the same for all taxpayers.

** Age allowances reduced by £1 for every £2 income in excess of the limit until the basic non-age-related allowance is reached – so if you earn £1000 over the limit your higher age-related personal allowance will be reduced by £500.

090110 000071 AA 000071

Inland Revenue

PAYE Coding Notice

This form shows your tax code for the tax year **1997–98**

Please keep all your coding notices. You may need to refer to them if you have to fill in a Tax Return.

846

MR A SMITH
1 THE STREET
THE TOWN
SHIRESHIRE
ABC1 CD2

HM INSPECTOR OF TAXES
LONDON PROVINCIAL 22 TSO
GRAYFIELD HOUSE
5 BANKHEAD AVENUE
SIGHTHILL
EDINBURGH EH11 4AE

Tax Office telephone ☎	Date of issue
0171 123 456	10 DEC 1997

Please quote your Tax reference and National Insurance number if you contact us

Tax reference	National Insurance number
456/ABC 1/D	NA 12 34 56 B

Your tax code for the year shown above is **K182**

This tax code is used to deduct tax payable on your income from

A COMPANY

If you move to another job, your new employer will normally continue to use this tax code.
The tax code is made up as follows:

The '*See note*' columns below refer to the numbered notes in the guidance leaflet P3 *Understanding Your Tax Code.* Leaflet P3 also tells you about the **letter part** of your tax code.

Check that the details are correct. If you think they are wrong, or you have any queries, contact your Tax Office (details above).

This coding notice replaces any previous notice for the year. You should pass it to your agent if you have one.

See note	Your tax allowances	£
10	JOB EXPENSES	30
01	PERSONAL ALLOWANCE	3765
02	WIFE'S MARRIED ALLOWANCE	1790
	Total allowances	5585

See note	Amounts taken away from your total allowances	£
30	CAR BENEFIT	5206
30	MEDICAL INSURANCE PAYMENTS	225
25	ALLOWANCE RESTRICTION	1118
39	TAX UNDERPAID £348.49	871
	Total deductions	7420

The Negative amount for the year is £ -1835 **, making your Tax Code** K182

See example overleaf

*The **Negative amount** is the difference between your **Total allowances** and **Total deductions**.*

PREVIOUS TAX CODE K252

If necessary we will use this box to give you further information about your tax code

Your tax code has changed. As soon as the new code is used, any refund due will be made by your wages or paying office.

The code is made up of numbers (usually three) and a letter, for example:

312H or K311

The figures in your Code show the amount you can earn in the tax year before paying tax.

When working out your Tax Code the last number is deleted. So if you can earn £4045 before paying tax your Code will have the number 404 (your Code number is one-tenth of your net allowances rounded down). The letter next to these numbers tells your employer what type of taxpayer you are.

The numbers

The Inland Revenue adds up your *allowances* including the personal allowance and married couple's allowance and may add on a sum to give you tax relief you are due for personal pension plan contributions, your mortgage (if it is not in the MIRAS scheme) or maintenance payments. You may also see a sum for job expenses – this is to ensure you are not taxed on expenses that are allowable and not taxable.

Then it adds up any deductions. You pay tax on your employee perks and benefits (such as your company car and private medical insurance) by an adjustment in your Tax Code. You are taxed on the value of these perks. Untaxed interest (interest received gross), tax on part-time earnings, taxable state benefits and property income can also be collected through your Tax Code, as can any outstanding tax from previous years.

The Inland Revenue subtracts the amount of *deductions* from the amount of *allowances* and gets a final figure. The last number is then knocked off. This is the number in your Tax Code.

The letters

These tell your employer how to treat your allowances and the type of taxpayer you are. This is what the most commonly used letters mean:

L You get the basic personal allowance.
H You get the personal allowance and the married couple's allowance.
P You get the higher age-related personal allowance for those aged between 65 and 74.
V You get the higher age-related married couple's allowance and higher personal allowance for those aged between 65 and 74.

T If you have a T code your tax will not be adjusted by your employer but by the Tax Office. You get a T code if: your age-related allowance is reduced because your income is more than the £15,600 limit; you are 75 and over during the tax year and get the higher age allowance and higher married couple's allowance; you don't want your employer to know your age or marital status.

K You get the K code if the value of any perks of your job and tax owed is greater than your personal allowances. The extra tax will be collected each month through PAYE, so you don't have to pay a big bill at the end of the tax year. See 'The K Code' below.

The 'K' code

This means you have a negative allowance, i.e. your deductions are greater than your allowances. It not only means that **all** your income is taxed (you have no tax-free allowance) but also that you have to pay an extra amount of tax from your salary. For example:

Mr K has total allowances of	**£4045**
His total deductions are	**£5050**
So he has a **negative** amount of allowance for the tax year of	**−£1005**

His code will be 100K.

The extra £1005 is added to his income before calculating the tax he must pay. As he is paid monthly the calculation is:

£1005 ÷ 12 = £84

So every month he will pay tax on **all** his salary plus tax on a further £84 will be deducted from his pay.

A booklet *Understanding Your Tax Code* which comes with your Coding Notice will explain how your Tax Code is worked out. If you still need further information, telephone the number on the top of your Coding Notice.

If you receive state benefits or a state pension

If you are taxed under PAYE and also receive taxable state benefits, any tax due on these will be collected through PAYE. So if you receive an employer's pension you may also have to pay taxes on your state pension and other benefits through your Tax Code.

TAX RELIEF

Tax relief reduces your tax bill by refunding tax you have already paid or by reducing the amount of tax you are liable to pay. Sometimes tax relief is given automatically so you do not notice that you are getting a rebate. In other cases you have to claim the tax relief on your Tax Return.

For example, if you are a higher-rate taxpayer you will get tax relief of 40p for every £1 you put in your pension. But you can only get tax relief at 40 per cent if you pay tax at 40 per cent and you have to have enough higher-rate earnings to qualify.

You are given this tax relief in your Tax Code by reducing the amount of earnings that fall into the higher rate tax bands. You automatically get basic-rate tax relief of 23 per cent when you pay your premiums.

There is also *reduced rate tax relief* which restricts the rate of tax relief – so even if you pay tax at 40 per cent you can only claim the tax relief at 15 per cent.

You don't always have to claim tax relief. Sometimes you get *tax relief at source.* Most mortgages come under MIRAS – *mortgage interest tax relief at source* – which means the mortgage lender will automatically give you tax relief on your mortgage payments up to the *tax relief limit* of £30,000 and will give you this tax relief at the correct reduced rate of 15 per cent (reducing to 10 per cent from April 1998). This tax relief means your mortgage payments are automatically reduced.

TAX AT SOURCE

Just as you can receive *tax relief at source,* you can also be taxed at source. This means that tax is already deducted before you receive your income.

This happens with your salary if you are an employee. Your employer will deduct tax under the PAYE (Pay-As-You-Earn) system using your Tax Code to work out how much of your earnings can be tax free.

Most bank and building society income is also taxed at source. But tax is deducted at 20 per cent. Only higher-rate taxpayers need to pay any additional tax. Basic 23 per cent tax payers do not need to pay any additional tax even though tax has been deducted at the lower rate.

The same applies to share dividends which are currently paid after 20 per cent tax has been deducted.

Non-taxpayers can currently reclaim the tax deducted or, in the case of savings accounts, ask their bank or building society to pay the interest gross (without tax deducted).

SUMMARY

⇒ The tax year covered by the Tax Return sent out in April 1988 runs from 6 April 1997 to 5 April 1998.

⇒ Everyone receives a basic personal allowance – this means that the first £4045 of your taxable income is exempt from tax. You may also qualify for additional tax allowances.

⇒ Your allowances can be reduced to take account of tax you owe. This will be done using your Tax Code.

⇒ Some types of income are tax free.

⇒ Some types of income are taxed at source.

⇒ Your *taxable income* is all your income (excluding tax-free income) after your tax allowances have been deducted.

⇒ The lower rate of tax is 20 per cent – you pay this on the first £4100 of taxable income (income in excess of your tax allowances).

⇒ The basic rate of tax is 23 per cent – you pay this on the next £22,000 of taxable income.

⇒ The higher rate of tax is 40 per cent and is paid on taxable income above £26,100.

4

TIPS ON FILLING IN YOUR TAX RETURN

⇒ You **must** fill in your Tax Return in blue or black ink. However, you are advised to use pencil to make it easier to correct any mistakes. Only when you are satisfied with the information you have given should you write over the pencil in ink.

⇒ Ignore pence when writing figures. This simply means that you should round all figures to the nearest pound.

⇒ **Everyone has to fill in pages 3 to 8 of the main Tax Return.** But you do not have to fill in every box – only the ones that relate to your financial circumstances.

⇒ Do not tick the ***NO*** boxes to say that you do not have to fill in a question until you have read through all the notes. For instance, you may not realize that all of your savings and investments are tax free and you do not have to fill in that section after all.

⇒ You should also have a calculator as some addition and subtraction may be required.

PART
2

STEP-BY-STEP GUIDE TO FILLING IN THE MAIN TAX RETURN

5

THE QUESTIONNAIRE

Read the cover and make sure that you fully understand what is required and that the information is correct.

Check that your title, name and address are correct. If they are wrong, simply amend any errors by deleting the information that is wrong and writing the correct information next to it.

Note your Tax Reference as you will need to refer to it in all correspondence with the Inland Revenue.

Note your Tax Office telephone number. This will be useful if you have any questions.

Read carefully through the instructions and note the deadlines for submitting your completed Tax Return.

Everyone has to fill in page 2 to make sure they have the right supplementary pages.

STEP 1: FILL IN THE QUESTIONNAIRE

Q1: Employment

Tick the ***yes*** box if you were employed at any time during the tax year 6 April 1997 to 5 April 1998.

> **Warning:** You may be classed as an employee even if you do casual work, do not have a contract of employment or even if you are normally self-employed.

Inland Revenue **Tax Return** *for the year ended 5 April 1998*

Official use 12345 67801
Tax Reference AB 12 3456C
Employer Reference ABE1

Date 7 April 1998

Tax Office address

Officer in Charge
LONDON PROVINCIAL 22
GRAYFIELD HOUSE
5 BANKHEAD AVENUE
EDINBURGH
EH11 4AE

MR A SMITH
1 THE STREET
THE TOWN
SHIRESHIRE
AB1 2DE

Please read this page first

The green arrows and instructions will guide you through your Tax Return.

This Notice requires you by law to send me a Tax Return for the year from 6 April 1997 to 5 April 1998. Give details of all your income and capital gains using:

- ***this form and any supplementary Pages you need, OR***
- ***other Inland Revenue approved forms, OR***
- ***the Electronic Lodgement Service (ELS).***

Make sure your Tax Return, and any documents asked for, reaches me by:

- *the later of **30 September 1998** and **2 months after the date this notice was given** if you want me to calculate your tax, **OR***
- *the later of **31 January 1999 and 3 months after the date this notice was given, at the latest**, or you will be liable to an automatic penalty of £100.*

Make sure your payment of any tax you owe reaches me by 31 January, or you will have to pay interest and perhaps a surcharge.

All Tax Returns will be checked. Please remember that there are penalties for supplying false information.

Your Tax Return

I have sent you pages 1 to 8 of your Tax Return:

- *page 2 tells you about supplementary Pages for some types of income and gains. For example, there are Pages for employment, and for self-employment income*
- *pages 3 and 4 are for details of other income, for example, pensions and savings*
- *page 5 is for claiming reliefs*
- *page 6 is for claiming allowances*
- *pages 7 and 8 are for other information.*

I have included any supplementary Pages I think you need after page 8. You are responsible for making sure you have the right ones. Use page 2 to check.

I have also sent you:

- *a Tax Return Guide to help you fill in your Tax Return (read pages 2 to 5 of the Guide before you start), and*
- *a Tax Calculation Guide to help you if you are calculating your own tax.*

If you need help:

- *refer to your Tax Return Guide, **OR***
- *ring the number above - most questions can be answered by telephone, **OR***
- *when the office is closed, phone our Helpline on 0645 000 444 for general advice. It is open each evening and at weekends, **OR***
- *if you do not want to explain your question on the phone, call in at a Tax Enquiry Centre - look under 'Inland Revenue' in the phone book.*

Please turn over

Inland Revenue **INCOME AND CAPITAL GAINS** *for the year ended 5 April 1998*

Step 1 Answer Questions 1 to 9 below to find out if you have the right supplementary Pages. Please read pages 6 and 7 of your Tax Return Guide if you need help. The Questions are colour coded to help you identify the supplementary Pages and their guidance notes. If you answer 'No', go to the next question. If you answer 'Yes', you must complete the relevant supplementary Pages. Turn to the back of your Tax Return to see if you have the right ones and look at the back of the Tax Return Guide to see if you have guidance Notes to go with them. **Ring the Orderline on 0645 000 404, or fax on 0645 000 604 for any you need (open 7 days a week between 8am and 10pm). If I have sent you any Pages you do not need, ignore them.**

Check to make sure you have the right supplementary Pages and then tick the box below.

	Question			Supplementary Pages
Q1	Were you an employee, or office holder, or director, or agency worker in the year ended 5 April 1998?	NO	YES	EMPLOYMENT YES
Q2	Did you have any taxable income from share options or share related benefits in the year? (This does not include dividends - they go in Question 10)	NO	YES	SHARE SCHEMES YES
Q3	Were you self-employed (but not in partnership)? (Tick 'Yes' if you were a Name at Lloyd's)	NO	YES	SELF-EMPLOYMENT YES
Q4	Were you in partnership?	NO	YES	PARTNERSHIP YES
Q5	Did you receive any rent or other income from land and property in the UK?	NO	YES	LAND & PROPERTY YES
Q6	Did you have any taxable income from overseas pensions or benefits, or from foreign companies or savings institutions, offshore funds or trusts abroad, or from land and property abroad or gains on foreign insurance policies?	NO	YES	
	Have you at any time made, or been associated with, a transfer of assets which has resulted in income becoming payable to a foreign entity or have you benefited in any way from such a transfer made by someone else?	NO	YES	
	Do you want to claim tax credit relief for foreign tax paid on foreign income or gains?	NO	YES	FOREIGN YES
Q7	Did you receive any income from any trust, settlement or estate of a deceased person?	NO	YES	TRUSTS ETC YES
Q8	Capital gains			
	• Have you disposed of your exempt only or main residence? If 'Yes', read page 7 of your Tax Return Guide to see if you need the Capital Gains Pages.	NO	YES	
	• Did you dispose of other chargeable assets worth more than £13,000 in total?	NO	YES	
	• Were your total chargeable gains more than £6,500? You may also need to fill in the Capital Gains Pages if you made a capital loss.	NO	YES	CAPITAL GAINS YES
Q9	Are you claiming that you were not resident, or not ordinarily resident, or not domiciled, in the UK, or dual resident in the UK and another country, for all or part of the year?	NO	YES	NON-RESIDENCE ETC YES

Step 2 **Please use blue or black ink to fill in your Tax Return and please do not include pence.** Round down, to the nearest pound, your income and capital gains and round up your tax credits and tax deductions.
Now fill in any supplementary Pages BEFORE going to Step 3.
Tick this box when you have filled in your supplementary Pages ☐

Step 3 Now fill in Questions 10 to 23. If you answer 'No' to a question, go to the next one. If you answer 'Yes', fill in the relevant boxes.

Remember

- You do not have to calculate your tax - I will do it for you if you send your Tax Return to me by 30 September. This will save you time and effort.
- The Tax Calculation Guide I have sent you will help if you decide to calculate the tax yourself.
- You do not have to wait until 30 September 1998, or 31 January 1999, to send me your Tax Return.

BMSD 12/97 Tax Return: page 2

⇒ If you are unsure about whether or not you were an employee, you will usually be if one of the following applies:
- Tax was deducted from your pay by your employer.
- You were employed by an agency or an agency arranged work for you.

⇒ If you are normally self-employed, some earnings may be still classed as earnings from employment if one or more of the following applies:
- You were paid for your time – not for providing goods or services.
- You worked from the premises of someone who you were working for or used their equipment.
- You earn most (generally more than 75 per cent) of your earnings from one source.

Q2: Share schemes

Before you tick either ***YES*** or ***NO*** box you must first find out if your income from share options or share schemes is *taxable*. If your share options are **not** taxable tick the ***NO*** box. Share option schemes are set up by your employer to enable you to buy shares in the company you work for. Your share options are **not** taxable if they were granted:

⇒ under an Inland Revenue approved savings-related share option scheme and your monthly contributions of no more than £250 are invested in a Save As You Earn (SAYE) account to buy the shares at the end of three or five years;

⇒ from an approved profit-sharing scheme with the shares held by trustees for three years;

⇒ under an approved executive share option scheme on or before 17 July 1995 **and** the option was exercised (you got the shares) between three and ten years after the option was granted **and** you did/do not take shares within three years of exercising (buying) other share options. If granted after 17 July 1995, the total value of all shares subject to option must **not** be more than £30,000 at the time these new options was granted;

⇒ you only received dividends from shares bought through a company share scheme.

Tick the ***YES*** box if:

- ⇒ You invested in a SAYE scheme and bought shares within three years and did so because the company you work for was sold or taken over;
- ⇒ your share options were **not** in an approved Inland Revenue share option scheme. Check on the scheme documents for the word 'approved';
- ⇒ you received payment for giving up, or not exercising, a share option;
- ⇒ your approved executive share options are taxable and do not meet the requirements listed above.

Q3: Self-employment

You must tick the ***YES*** box if you were self-employed at any time during the tax year from 6 April 1997 to 5 April 1998.

Warning: You may have received earnings from self-employment even though you do not think of yourself as being self-employed. Read the following notes.

- ⇒ You were self-employed if you worked for yourself – carried on a trade, profession or vocation – arranging your own work, deciding when you work, providing your own tools and equipment and invoicing someone else or another business for the work you have done.
- ⇒ You may also be classed as self-employed if you received payments from a company – other than the one you are employed by – without tax being deducted from this income. For instance, you may have been given commission for introducing business to a company.
- ⇒ You can be self-employed and an employee.
- ⇒ If you make money out of your hobby – for instance, you buy cars, repair them and sell them on for a profit – you may also be classed as self-employed as you are carrying out a trade.
- ⇒ Note directors are employees, not self-employed.

Tip: If your freelance, casual or consultancy earning are 'one-offs' – for instance, you wrote one paid article for a trade magazine – you can include this income on your main tax return in box ***Q13.***

Q4: Partnerships

You will know if you are or were a partner of a business at any time during the tax year from 6 April 1997 to 5 April 1998 as you should have drawn up or signed a partnership agreement stating how the profits of the partnership are to be split.

Q5: Land and property

Some income from land and property does **not** have to be included in this section.

⇒ If you run a bed and breakfast business or rent out rooms and provide extra services such as meals in your only or main home, your activities will amount to a trade and as such you should tick the ***NO*** box. These come under self-employment.
⇒ Even if you are making the most of the Rent a Room relief – which allows you to rent a room in your home for up to £4250 a year and get that income tax free – you should tick the ***YES*** box.
⇒ If you receive rent from letting out your overseas or holiday home this is covered in the foreign income section – this section only covers UK land and property.

Q6: Foreign

This includes any overseas pensions or benefits, income from foreign companies or savings institutions, offshore funds or overseas trusts, rents from land and property, foreign life insurance policies and annuities.

⇒ If you invest in a UK unit trust or investment trust that in turn invests in overseas companies, this is **not** classed as foreign earnings.

⇒ Tick the ***YES*** box if you want to claim relief for foreign tax that has been deducted on any income or gains – this includes tax deducted by overseas savings institutions.

⇒ Tick the ***YES*** box if you received income from renting out your overseas home.

Q7: Trusts

The ***YES*** box must be ticked if you were a beneficiary or received money from a trust fund or you created (were the settlor of) a trust. But if you received a legacy in trust (from the estate of a deceased person) tick the ***NO*** box.

⇒ If you receive income from a 'nominee' account which is also known as a bare trust do not include this here. For tax purposes the income and profits belong to the beneficiary and not to the trust. Include this income on the relevant pages of your main Tax Return – so shares in a 'nominee' account should be included in the investment section.

Q8: Capital gains

Before you can tick the ***YES*** or ***NO*** boxes you have to know what capital gains tax is. It is a tax on profits when you sell investments, businesses or land. Instead of being taxed on the income (income tax) you are taxed on the profits (capital gains) when you sell an asset for more than you bought it for.

Did you sell your home?

Your only or main home is usually exempt from capital gains tax. But if you sold your home during the tax year you must still tick the ***YES*** box. But this does **not** mean that you have to pay Capital Gains Tax or that you have to fill in the Capital Gains form. You only have to do this if you sold some land adjoining your home, sold part of your property, earned money from your home by renting it out or used your home for running a business. Even in these cases you may be able to escape Capital Gains Tax. Read Chapter 20 for more details.

Did you dispose of other chargeable assets worth more than £13,000 in total?

You will only know the answer to this if you know what *chargeable assets* are. The following guidelines should help.

⇒ Stocks and shares, land, second homes, antiques and works of art. Most assets that are an investment are included.

⇒ You do **not** have to declare: personal possessions or chattels (which are each worth £6000 or less when you 'dispose' of them), gains from selling your car (unless you sell cars for a business), Personal Equity Plans (PEPs), bonuses from TESSA accounts, gilts (UK government stocks), foreign currency for personal use, betting and lottery winnings, most life insurance policies and some National Savings Investments. And if you are running a business, trading stock that you sell is also exempt.

⇒ The £13,000 applies to the total value of these items sold or disposed of during the tax year, not to each individual item.

⇒ The Inland Revenue uses the word 'dispose' rather than sold because you must also declare assets given as gifts or exchanged.

Were your gains/profits more than £6500?

This means that you sold your chargeable assets or investments at a profit – and that the profit from **all** the items you sold is more than £6500.

⇒ To work out the 'gain' or profit, deduct the price you paid for the asset from the price you sold it for. See Chapter 20 on Capital Gains Tax for other items you can deduct to reduce your gain.

⇒ Remember the £6500 limit is for your total gains, not each individual gain.

⇒ If you made a loss on selling an asset you should also fill in the Capital Gains Tax section so that you can offset these losses against any capital gains in this tax year or in the next tax year.

Q9: Non residence

This will apply to you if you live abroad or lived most of the tax year in another country. If you have not lived or worked overseas tick the ***NO*** box if.

- ⇒ You spent less than 183 days in the UK in the tax year, and over four years an average of less than 91 days, or have spent the entire year overseas.
- ⇒ You are living in the UK but come from overseas.

STEP 2: FILL IN THE SUPPLEMENTARY PAGES

Only fill in those pages that you have ticked **YES** in boxes **Q1** to **Q9**. If you ticked a box – for example self-employment – but do not have the right supplementary pages then ring the Orderline on 0645 000 404 and ask for any missing forms.

As you only have to fill in those forms that relate to your individual circumstances and these will vary from reader to reader, guidance on how to fill in these pages is given later in this book following the step-by-step guide to filling in the main pages of your Tax Return.

However, you are strongly advised to fill in the supplementary pages **before** filling in the rest of the main eight pages of your Tax Return. If you do not you may not be able to fill in these pages correctly.

Once you have filled in all your supplementary pages, tick the ***Step 2*** box on page 2 of your Tax Return.

STEP 3: FILL IN THE MAIN TAX RETURN

A step-by-step guide to filling in **Q10** to **Q16** is given in the next few chapters.

Remember: The Tax Return states 'ignore pence'. This simply means that you can round all income figures down. For instance, instead of writing £109.55 you simply write £109. Do not round up to £110 unless it works to your advantage – so round up your outgoings.

6

SAVINGS INTEREST AND SHARE DIVIDENDS

PAPERWORK REQUIRED

It is essential that you have all the paperwork you need **before** filling in page 3 of the main Tax Return:

- ❑ bank and building society passbooks and any annual statements;
- ❑ unit trust and investment trust statements;
- ❑ National Savings documents;
- ❑ any other savings and investment literature you have;
- ❑ share dividend tax vouchers.

> **Remember:** You only need information about income received in the 6 April 1997 to 5 April 1998 tax year.

What if I don't have all the paperwork?

- ❑ **Savings.** Ask your bank or building society to send you a tax deduction certificate. These annual statements are sent out automatically to those with larger savings. Or you can try to work out the interest you have earned, but it may be difficult calculating how much interest falls in the tax year.
- ❑ **Share dividends.** These should be paid to you with a tax voucher attached. If you have lost these, ask the company share registrar for a duplicate.

❑ **Unit trusts and investment trusts.** You should ask the investment company for a duplicate of your annual statement.

Q10: Savings and investments

INCOME *for the year ended 5 April 1998*

Q10 **Did you receive any income from UK savings and investments?** NO ☐ YES ☐ If yes, fill in boxes 10.1 to 10.32 as appropriate. Include only your share from any joint savings and investments.

Some savings accounts and share dividends are not taxable and as such do **not** have to be listed on your Tax Return. Note that even if tax **has** already been deducted from taxable savings and investments, you must still tick the ***YES*** box.

Although the question says did you 'receive any income' – this does not only mean that you actually received the money by taking income out of a savings or investment account or scheme. If your account was credited with interest or you earned income or interest that was then reinvested in your unit trust or other investment scheme, that **must** also be included.

Do not tick the ***YES*** box if **all** your interest and dividend income is included in the following list.

Tax-free income from savings and investments

⇒ Personal Equity Plan (PEP) investments such as shares, unit trusts or investment trusts. However, if you have withdrawn more than £180 interest earned a cash help in the PEP you will have to declare this.

⇒ The first £70 of interest from a National Savings Ordinary Account.

⇒ Income from tax-free National Savings schemes:
- Fixed Interest Savings Certificates;
- Index-Linked Savings Certificates;
- Children's Bonus Bonds;
- Any winnings from Premium Bonds.

⇒ TESSAs – Tax Exempt Special Savings Accounts – providing you keep your money invested for at least five years.

⇒ SAYE – Save as You Earn – accounts. These were withdrawn from 1 December 1994 although you can still invest in them to buy shares in the company you work for. If you still have a scheme, it is tax free.

⇒ Dividends from ordinary shares in venture capital trusts.

Important:

- ❑ **For those with joint accounts and joint investments.** If you have a savings account or shares in a joint name only include **your** share of the income. This will usually be half. However, you can elect to split income differently but you must tell the Inland Revenue first. If you want to split income differently make a note in the Additional information box on page 8.
- ❑ **For those who receive gross interest (without tax already deducted).** These are accounts that pay interest *gross*, which means **no** tax is deducted 'at source' by the bank or building society. Remember, just because interest is paid gross does not mean that it is not taxable.
- ❑ **For those with more than one investment.** If you have several building society accounts, unit trusts or share investments you must add up the total amount of each type of income before filling in each box. There is a blank form for you to use on page 28 of the Revenue Tax Return guide.
- ❑ **If you stopped receiving interest from a particular source in the 1996/97 tax year you may have paid too much tax.** See page 9 of the Revenue tax return guide for more details.

HOW TO WORK OUT THE GROSS AMOUNT ON TAXED INTEREST AND DIVIDENDS

Gross simply means the amount before tax is deducted. To get this figure add together the *net* amount (the amount you received after tax) and the tax that was deducted. If you do not know how much tax has been deducted you will have to do a simple calculation. Tax is deducted at 20 per cent on savings interest and share dividends. But to find out how much tax has been deducted you must multiply the amount of interest by 25 per cent.

So if you earned £100 of gross interest:

20% tax x £100 = £20

£20 tax deducted from £100 gross interest = £80 net interest.

If you received £80 of net interest:

£80 x 25% (or divide by 4) = £20 tax deducted

£80 net interest + £20 tax = £100 gross interest.

INTEREST

	Amount after tax deducted	Tax deducted	Taxable amount / Gross amount before tax
• Interest from UK banks, building societies and deposit takers			
- where **no tax** has been deducted			Taxable amount: 10.1 £
- where **tax has** been deducted	10.2 £ 480	10.3 £ 120	Gross amount before tax: 10.4 £ 600
• Interest distributions from UK authorised unit trusts and open-ended investment companies (dividend distributions go below)	10.5 £	10.6 £	Gross amount before tax: 10.7 £
• National Savings (other than FIRST Option Bonds and the first £70 of interest from a National Savings Ordinary Account)			Taxable amount: 10.8 £
• National Savings FIRST Option Bonds	10.9 £	10.10 £	Gross amount before tax: 10.11 £
• Other income from UK savings and investments (except dividends)	10.12 £	10.13 £	Gross amount before tax: 10.14 £

Box 10.1:

If you have any interest that is paid gross (without tax deducted), this should be totalled up and the amount written in box **10.1**.

Boxes 10.2 to 10.4:

See the notes on page 38 on how to calculate the gross amount before tax.

Boxes 10.5 to 10.7:

Only include unit trust interest payments, **not** dividends. If you received interest with no tax deducted simply enter '0' in box 10.6. Remember that even if you did not actually receive any interest but it was used to buy more units or shares, you must still show the amount of interest you earned. Do not include any PEP investments unless you withdrew more than £180 interest from cash that had not yet been invested by your PEP manager. Do not include any 'equalization' payments as these are simply repayments of capital and therefore are not classed as income.

Box 10.8:

Do not include National Savings schemes that are not taxable – such as Savings Certificates (see the list on page 37). And don't forget to deduct the first £70 of interest if you have an Ordinary Account. If you do not know how much interest has been earned, send your book away to have it added. Include interest from the Ordinary Account, Investment Account, Deposit Bonds, Income Bonds and Pensioners' Guaranteed Income Bonds. Show the interest added to Capital Bonds during the year. Don't forget that tax is **not** deducted at source from the National Savings Schemes, so do not gross up your interest.

Boxes 10.9 to 10.11:

First Option Bonds are paid with tax already deducted. So you will need to gross up the amount and insert the amount of tax deducted.

Boxes 10.12 to 10.14:

Include any other interest you have earned that has not been entered into any of the other boxes. This will include interest from government stocks (gilts) including those bought through the National Savings Stock Register, interest on loans to individuals or organisations and interest from credit unions and friendly societies. If no tax has been deducted, fill in the gross amount and do **not** work out how much tax should be deducted – or the Inland Revenue will assume you have already paid tax on this interest.

If you received income from an annuity (a lump-sum investment scheme that provides you with an income) and that annuity was **not** linked to a pension you will have to include that income in these boxes. Some of your income will be exempt as it is simply a repayment of your capital.

These boxes should also be used for those who have invested in discounted securities such as discounted bonds. See the Inland Revenue guidance notes and ask your financial adviser for further advice and information.

DIVIDENDS

• Dividends and other qualifying distributions from UK companies	Dividend/distribution 10.15 £ 224	Tax credit 10.16 £ 56	Dividend/distribution plus credit 10.17 £ 280
• Dividend distributions from UK authorised unit trusts and open-ended investment companies	Dividend/distribution 10.18 £	Tax credit 10.19 £	Dividend/distribution plus credit 10.20 £
• Scrip dividends from UK companies	Dividend 10.21 £	Notional tax 10.22 £	Dividend plus notional tax 10.23 £
• Foreign income dividends from UK companies	Dividend 10.24 £	Notional tax 10.25 £	Dividend plus notional tax 10.26 £
• Foreign income dividend distributions from UK authorised unit trusts and open-ended investment companies	Dividend 10.27 £	Notional tax 10.28 £	Dividend plus notional tax 10.29 £
• Non-qualifying distributions and loans written off	10.30 £	Notional tax 10.31 £	Taxable amount 10.32 £

Boxes 10.15 to 10.17:

Simply copy the information from your share dividend vouchers. Dividends are the income you receive on shares. Do not include foreign income dividends or scrip dividends (where you receive extra shares instead of a cash dividend). Note that investment trusts are UK stock market quoted companies so you should put your dividend details in these boxes, unless you invested via a PEP.

Boxes 10.18 to 10.20:

These boxes are for dividends from unit trusts and a newer type of collective investment scheme known as OEICs (open-ended investment companies) which are similar to unit trusts. Remember that even if your dividends were used to buy more units or shares you are still treated as though you earned these dividends and must declare them. Your money will be reinvested in this way if you have purchased 'accumulation' units. Do not include any 'equalization' payments as these are repayments of capital and are therefore not classed as income.

Boxes 10.21 to 10.23:

If you take shares instead of a cash dividend this is known as a scrip dividend. These are taxed in the same way as other dividends and you are taxed on 'the appropriate amount in cash'. This is paid after tax so write the amount in box **10.21** and work out the notional tax (by dividing by 4 or multiplying by 25 per cent) and add these figures together and write the total in box **10.23**.

Boxes 10.24 to 10.29:

The same rules apply as for UK dividends and unit trusts. If the dividends are foreign your dividend voucher will show the amounts.

Boxes 10.30 to 10.32:

Non-qualifying distributions include bonus or redeemable shares and loans written off by companies. See your Tax Return Guide for more information.

HOW TO USE THE INFORMATION IN QUESTION 10 TO SAVE TAX

Now that you have filled in the answers to **Q10** you can look at ways to reorganise your finances to save tax. Unfortunately you cannot make tax savings for the 1997/98 tax year as that has already ended. But you can save tax for future years.

Tax tips:

- ☐ If you are married and one partner is a higher-rate taxpayer, the other a non-taxpayer or paying tax at the lower or basic rate, you will save tax by putting all or most of the investment into the name of the partner who pays the least tax. You cannot backdate the way you split income so you will not save tax on your April 1998 Tax Return as the change only takes place from the date you make a declaration. Ask your Tax Office for advice and for Form 17. If you put all of your investments into the name of the partner who pays the least tax this must be an outright 'gift'. Otherwise the Inland Revenue may believe that you have not actually transferred the investment. By splitting your investments you can also save on capital gains tax – particularly if one partner does not use up all of their Capital Gains Tax allowance or pays the tax at a lower rate.

- ❑ Some £764 million of tax is wasted by unit trust, investment trust and share investors who do not make the most of PEPs – Personal Equity Plans. You can invest up to £6000 in a main PEP and £3000 in a single-share PEP this year and no Income Tax is payable on dividends or other income and you can sell your investment free of Capital Gains Tax. Although these will be withdrawn in April 1999 and replaced by the Individual Savings Account, PEP investments can be rolled over into the new scheme and all savings will still be free of Income and Capital Gains Tax.
- ❑ Consider tax-free savings schemes. Currently only TESSAs – the Tax-Exempt Special Savings Account – and some National Savings schemes are available. TESSAs must be held for a minimum of five years and will be replaced in April 1999 by the new Individual Savings Account. You will be able to transfer your money into the ISA but watch out for any penalties or loss of bonuses.
- ❑ Income from savings and share dividends is taxed at 20 per cent with this tax deducted from your interest on dividends before they are paid to you. But basic-rate taxpayers who pay tax at 23 per cent do **not** have to pay an extra 3 per cent so make a tax saving. However, higher-rate taxpayers must pay the full 40 per cent tax so must pay an extra 20 per cent tax on top of that already deducted. Remember, your savings income is **added** to all your other income when working out your tax. This means that interest and dividends can push you into the higher-rate tax bracket.
- ❑ If you do not need your investment income, consider switching your investments into schemes that give you capital growth rather than income. This is because most or all of the investment will be taxed under Capital Gains Tax, which taxes the profits you make when you sell an investment instead of the income you earn from that investment. The allowance for Capital Gains is far higher than that for Income Tax – £6500 for the 1997/98 tax year. Many taxpayers fail to use up this allowance and provided your total profit from sales of investments and other assets is less than £6500 you will pay no tax.
- ❑ Offshore investments earn interest gross (without tax deducted). Although you must declare this income, you may not have to pay tax on it until nine months after the end of the tax year. You can therefore reinvest your interest and earn interest on this interest to boost your return. The same applies to dividends.
- ❑ If you want to boost your savings rate, consider a local authority bond, also known as a yearly bond. Investments start at £1000. However, if you sell your investment before the six-monthly interest payment is made, you should make a capital gain rather than earning interest and therefore will escape any Income Tax. However, this only applies if the nominal value of these does not exceed £5000. The same rules apply to gilts if you convert interest into capital if sold 'cum interest'.

Tax warning: If you put savings into your children's name or into a children's account and the child is under 18 you – as the parent – may have to pay tax. If the interest is above £100 gross a year you will pay tax on the whole income (not just the proportion above £100). The same applies if you set up a *trust* fund to pay income to your children. To get round this rule, a grandparent or aunt and uncle can set up a savings or investment scheme for your child and the child will not pay tax, unless income exceeds the personal allowance of £4045.

7

PENSIONS, SOCIAL SECURITY BENEFITS, MAINTENANCE PAYMENTS AND OTHER INCOME

PAPERWORK REQUIRED

- ❑ Details of any state benefits or pensions you received.
- ❑ Your P60, if you receive a company pension.
- ❑ Details of any income taken from a personal pension plan.
- ❑ Records of how much you received from any annuities purchased to give you an income for life.

Q11: State pensions and benefits

■ ***State pensions and benefits***	Tax deducted	Taxable amount for 1997-98
• State Retirement Pension		11.1 £
• Widow's Pension		11.2 £
• Widowed Mother's Allowance		11.3 £
• Industrial Death Benefit Pension		11.4 £
• Jobseeker's Allowance		11.5 £
• Invalid Care Allowance		11.6 £
• Statutory Sick Pay and Statutory Maternity Pay paid by the Department of Social Security		11.7 £
	Tax deducted	Gross amount before tax
• Taxable Incapacity Benefit	11.8 £	11.9 £

Many state benefits are **not** taxable and as such do **not** need to be included on your Tax Return.

Taxable state benefits include:

- ❑ state retirement pension and widow's pension;
- ❑ widowed mother's allowance;
- ❑ industrial death benefit pension;
- ❑ Jobseeker's Allowance;
- ❑ invalid care allowance;
- ❑ statutory sick pay and statutory maternity pay (only include in this section if paid by the Department of Social Security – if paid by the employer it will be included in your total pay for the year and tax will have been deducted by your employer);
- ❑ taxable incapacity benefit.

Tick the ***YES*** box if you received any of the above benefits **and/or** if you received **any** other pension.

Boxes 11.1 to 11.9:

This section is very straightforward. There are only two things you must take care over.

1. You must enter the full amount you were *entitled to* in the tax year from 6 April 1997 to 5 April 1998. So if you receive a payment quarterly or monthly, do not add up the equivalent amount over a year. The figure you give must be for the tax year only. So if you receive a payment on 10 April and some of this included benefits or pensions before 6 April, you must exclude the amount payable for the pre-6 April period.
2. You must ensure you do not include any non-taxable benefits.

If you are not sure what figures to include or want to check the figures you can ask the Benefit Office (part of the Department of Social Security) for a statement of taxable state benefits you have received.

If you received a combined payment from the Benefit Office, ask for this to be broken down into component parts. For instance, if your Income Support includes your pension and attendance allowance, ask for this to be split into separate amounts so that your attendance allowance is not taxed.

A full list of what should be included in this section is given on page 13 of your Inland Revenue guidance notes.

Box 11.1:

State pensions include:

- basic pension;
- State Earnings Related Pension (SERPS);
- graduated pension;
- age addition if you are over 80;
- incapacity addition or addition for dependent adult;
- any increases paid by the DSS to uprate a guaranteed minimum pension.

Do not include the Christmas bonus or any increase in pension for a dependent child.

If you receive a war widow's pension or are a dependant of a deceased former member of the Forces or Merchant Navy, ask for Help Sheet IR310 from the Orderline on 0645 000 404. This will tell you if you can receive your pension tax free and, if not, how much tax you need to pay.

> **Remember:** Pensions received from another country must be included on the foreign pages.

Boxes 11.2 to 11.7:

Simply enter the total amount you were entitled to in the tax year.

Boxes 11.8 to 11.9:

The reason why you are asked to include the tax deducted is that some Incapacity Benefits are taxable. However, payments in the first 28 weeks of in-capacity it are **not** taxable. Ask the Department of Social Security for details and figures.

Q11: Other pensions and retirement annuities

	Amount after tax deducted	Tax deducted	Gross amount before tax
• Pensions (other than State pensions) and retirement annuities	11.10 £	11.11 £	11.12 £

	Amount of deduction
• Deduction - see the note for box 11.3 on page 14 of your Tax Return Guide	11.13 £

These include:

- ❑ pensions from your former employer or your late spouse's former employer's company pension scheme;
- ❑ personal pension plans – including income withdrawals where no annuity has been purchased;
- ❑ income from any additional pension from free-standing additional voluntary contributions (FSAVCs). But refunds of surplus AVCs should go in boxes **12.10** to **12.12**. These will be refunds because you have paid in more than is allowed as a percentage of your income;
- ❑ income from retirement annuity contracts (an annuity is purchased from your personal pension fund on retirement to provide you with an income for life).

Purchased life annuities (lump-sum investments that give you an income for the rest of your life) which are **not** linked to a pension should also be included in boxes **11.10** to **11.12**.

Boxes 11.10 to 11.12:

If you receive a pension from an occupational pension scheme (from a former employer's scheme) this will be paid to you with tax already deducted, in the same way as salaries are paid after PAYE. You should be sent a form P60 by 31 May 1998 showing you how much was paid in the tax year and how much tax was deducted.

Income from a Personal Pension Plan (when you retire your fund is used to buy an annuity to give you an income) should also be included. If you have not yet purchased an annuity, any income taken out of your pension fund should be included. Ask your plan provider for details of income received. As with employer pensions, income is taxed at source under PAYE for personal pensions and with basic rate tax deducted from retirement annuity contracts.

Total up all the pensions before filling in the boxes. Do **not** include any lump sums you received on retirement as these are usually tax free.

Box 11.13:

You will only need to fill in this box if:

- you worked for an overseas government or are a dependant or widow of someone who did;
- your pension was increased because you retired on the grounds of disability by work injury or because of a work-related illness;
- your pension is paid for war injuries or other disability incurred while in military service.

See page 14 of your Tax Return Guide for further information.

Tax tips:

- If you are coming up to retirement and do not need to take your pension you can defer it and take it at a later date. Not only will this boost your income later on (when you might need the extra money) but you can defer paying tax on the pension until you receive it. So if you have a high income now and will have a much lower income later on, you will be taxed on your state pension or company pension at a lower rate.
- When you retire you can take a tax-free lump sum from your pension. This can be a maximum of 25 per cent of the fund if you have a personal pension or one-third of your final pay if you are in a final-salary company pension scheme. You may be better off investing this cash in a tax-free savings scheme than purchasing an annuity which is taxable or using the lump sum to reduce any loans or mortgages.

Q12: Maintenance received and gains on life insurance policies

This section covers a wide range of extras.

PAPERWORK REQUIRED

- ❑ Details of any maintenance or alimony payments you received and documents detailing the court orders, Child Support Agency or other agreements made.
- ❑ Details of any taxable UK life insurance policies (your life insurance company or friendly society should have sent you a chargeable event certificate).
- ❑ Details of any refunds of surplus additional voluntary contributions (the top-up pension schemes linked to your company pension scheme).

	Income receivable	Exempt amount	Income less exempt amount
• Taxable maintenance or alimony	12.1 £ 3000	12.2 £ 1830	12.3 £ 1170

Boxes 12.1 to 12.3: Taxable maintenance or alimony

Not all maintenance income **received** from a former spouse or your parents is taxable. If you receive *voluntary* maintenance payments or payments under an agreement or *court order* made **on or after 15 March 1988** you are covered by the 'new rules' and do **not** have to pay any tax on what you receive and you do not have to include these payments on your Tax Return.

Different or 'old rules' apply to maintenance payments agreed or made by court order **before 15 March 1988**. These maintenance payments are taxable but you won't have to pay tax on all the maintenance payments you receive.

Boxes 12.1 to 12.3:

Only fill these boxes in if you come under the 'old rules', i.e. your maintenance payments were agreed before 15 March 1988. Agreed maintenance payments include those:

- ❑ made under a court order (the 15 March 1988 deadline is extended to 30 June 1988 if the application to the court was made before 15 March 1988);
- ❑ Child Support Agency (CSA) assessments (provided the Inland Revenue was informed of the pre-15 March 1988 agreement by 30 June 1988);

- written and verbal agreements (provided the Inland Revenue received details of these by 30 June 1988);
- court orders, assessments and written agreements made after 15 March 1988 but only varying or adding to any pre-15 March 1988 payments.

Do **not** fill in this box if:

- the payments are voluntary (regardless of when they were first paid);
- you are over 21 and receive maintenance payments from your parents;
- the person making the payments has written to you stating they have made an election for the 'new rules' to apply.

If your maintenance payments have increased, only write in the amount you were due to receive in the 6 April 1988 to 5 April 1989 tax year in box **12.1**. You do not have to pay tax on any maintenance payments above this amount.

If you receive less now than you did in the 1988/89 tax year, you will pay tax on the lower amount. So write the amount you received in the 1997/98 tax year in box **12.1.**

In some cases *the first £1830 of maintenance payments is free of tax.* Anything over this sum is taxable. You will qualify for the tax allowance if:

- the payments are from your separated or former spouse;
- they are for yourself or for the support of a child aged under 21;
- you have **not** remarried;
- during the 1997/98 tax year you did not live with the separated or former spouse who pays the maintenance.

Note: The payments can only be paid to the spouse; payments to children or stepchildren are taxable on the full amount.

The exempt amount in box **12.2** will either be the £1830 tax-free allowance or the amount you received if this is lower. The amount over this sum should be written in box **12.39** and the total amount received in box **12.1**.

Tax tips:

- ❑ If your maintenance payments have been increased since 6 April 1989 you do not have to pay tax on the extra amounts.
- ❑ Try to get your former spouse to elect that the payments be treated under the 'new rules' as qualifying maintenance payments. Under the 'new rules' you will not pay any tax. However, your separated or former spouse may lose out. The payer can claim an Income Tax reduction on the amount he or she pays up to a maximum of the married couple's allowance (£1900 from April 1998). But he or she will only receive tax relief at 10 per cent from April 1998 and will no longer be able to claim tax relief at his or her higher rate. But if you receive maintenance you will gain.

If you want more information ask for leaflet *IR93: Separation, divorce and maintenance payments* by ringing the Orderline on 0645 000 404.

Boxes 12.4 to 12.9: Gains on UK Life Insurance policies

	Number of years	Notional tax	Amount of gain
• Gains on UK life insurance policies (without notional tax)	12.4		12.5 £
• Gains on UK life insurance policies (with notional tax)	12.6	12.7 £	12.8 £

Do not think you have to fill this in just because your life insurance policy has matured (paid out). Most life insurance policies are **not** taxable.

To be exempt from tax you must have a *qualifying policy.* This simply means that it qualifies as being tax exempt. These are policies which require you to pay premiums monthly or annually for at least ten years. However, don't think the returns are completely tax free. The insurance company has to pay tax on its profits (unless it is a friendly society). Your policy is treated as though you have paid basic rate tax. This is known as *notional* tax. Even if you are a non-taxpayer you cannot reclaim this tax.

Non-qualifying policies are generally single-premium policies – where you make a one-off investment. They are not bought as life insurance policies but as investments and are often called investment bonds.

You will pay tax on the difference between what is paid out (the maturity proceeds) and the amount you paid in (the premiums paid). Some of these policies allow you to make 5 per cent withdrawals every year. The life assurance company will give you a 'chargeable event' certificate showing that a potentially taxable withdrawal has been made.

However, some *qualifying* policies may also be taxable. If you cash in a policy before ten years are up, provided you have been paying regular premiums for at least three-quarters of the term of the policy or ten years (whichever is the lower) your gain remains tax free. If you cash in the policy before then, your policy is treated as a *non-qualifying* policy and you will be taxed. This is why you have to write the number of years you have held the policy on your Tax Return.

If you are in doubt as to whether your policy is taxable or not, ask your insurance company.

You may also be taxed on a non-qualifying policy if you:

- ❑ make a partial withdrawal from your policy;
- ❑ payments are made on death;
- ❑ you take out a loan against your policy from the insurance company; or
- ❑ you sell your policy.

Only add up gains from policies if you bought a cluster of identical policies with identical gains. Otherwise you must include details of **all** policies in the 'Additional information' box on page 8 of your Tax Return and then add up the total gains and put them in boxes **12.5**, **12.7** and **12.8**. Do not fill in boxes **12.4** or **12.6**.

Note: Do not include any gains from foreign policies. These go on the foreign pages.

Boxes 12.4 and 12.5:

These boxes are for friendly society policies and certain life annuities that are not treated as having being taxed at the basic rate. Write the number of **complete years** not part years that you have held your policy for in the first box. If, in the past, you have made part-withdrawals, part-sale or taken out a loan against the policy, write the number of complete years since then. To work out your gain deduct the premiums from the amount you received.

Boxes 12.6 to 12.8:

This is for gains from life insurance policies bought from companies that pay tax on their life insurance funds. As explained above, *notional* tax at 23 per cent is deducted. Again write in the number of complete years – or complete years since the last part-withdrawal, loan or part-sale.

For more information ask for Help Sheet *IR320: Gains on UK life insurance policies.*

Tax tips:

- Basic rate taxpayers do not have to pay any additional tax on taxable gains from life insurance polices, life annuities and capital redemption polices. You only have to pay tax at 40 per cent if you are a higher-rate taxpayer. This is because life insurance policies are treated as though they have already been taxed at the basic rate. So, if you are considering making a part or full withdrawal, select a year when you are a basic rate taxpayer.
- If you have a non-qualifying investment bond you can usually take out 5 per cent of the fund each year without paying tax at the time. But at the end of the policy, the amount you have withdrawn will be added to the gain to work out the tax due. So if you are then a lower-rate taxpayer (for instance you have retired) there will be no extra tax to pay. If you do not withdraw the full 5 per cent each year, you can carry this amount forward (use this allowance in future years).
- The proceeds of a taxable life insurance policy or investment bond may push you into the 40 per cent tax bracket. This is because the income you receive is added to your total income and only then is your top rate of tax calculated. If you only pay higher-rate tax because of the life insurance gain, you can reduce the amount of tax you pay using *top-slicing relief*. This means that you work out your average yearly gain over the number of years that the policy ran. You add this average yearly gain to your 1997/98 income. If you no longer fall into the higher-rate tax bracket once this is added to your other income, you will not have to pay higher-rate tax. Or you may find that you only have a small amount of income in the higher-rate tax bracket, so you only have to pay 40 per cent tax on part of your gain.

  The reason why you get this tax concession is that the gains in boxes **12.5** and **12.8** do not take into account the fact that gains may have accrued over a number of years. However, you cannot use top-slicing relief to increase your age-related allowances by reducing your total income.

  You will need a separate Tax Calculation Guide SA154 for this and should **not** use the standard calculation guide SA151.

HOW TO CALCULATE NOTIONAL TAX

Most life companies will have already paid tax on their profits, capital gains and income from investments. This is the 'notional' tax that you have effectively paid on your life insurance policy. To work it out simply deduct 23 per cent of the amount you receive (the figure in box **12.8**) and write this in the notional tax box. Friendly societies do not have to pay notional tax so include the gain in box **12.5.** If you are unsure whether notional tax has been deducted or not, ask your investment adviser or the life insurance/ investment company. You may have been sent a chargeable event certificate showing gains you have made and tax paid.

Box 12.9:

This will only apply if you have made taxable withdrawals during the term of the policy. You must include the amount so that the total amount taxed as investment income is not more than the total gain.

Boxes 12.10 to 12.12: Surplus additional voluntary contributions

	Amount received	Notional tax	Amount plus notional tax
• Refunds of surplus additional voluntary contributions	12.10 £	12.11 £	12.12 £

When you pay into a company pension scheme you receive tax relief at your top rate of tax. That is 40p for every £1 you invest if you are a higher-rate taxpayer. However, this tax break is restricted. You can only pay in 15 per cent of your earnings if you are in a company scheme and your pension on retirement cannot exceed two-thirds of final salary subject to an earnings cap of £84,000, rising to £87,600 from April 1998.

If you have paid in more than allowed and exceeded the limits on retirement, enter the total amount of the surplus AVC (not the amount of refund you received) in box **12.12**, the amount of refund you actually received after tax in box **12.10** and the tax deducted in box **12.11**.

Surplus additional voluntary contributions are refunded after 33 per cent tax is deducted (the 1997/98 tax rate). Basic rate tax payers cannot reclaim this and higher rate tax payers need to pay additional tax.

Q13: Other income

PAPERWORK REQUIRED

- ❑ Details of any income not included anywhere else on your tax return.
- ❑ Records of any isolated casual, freelance or artistic income.
- ❑ Details of any patent rights you have sold for a capital lump sum.
- ❑ Annual payments from UK unauthorized unit trusts.
- ❑ Annual payments paid by former employers which are not pension payments.

This is a chance for you to include anything you have not been able to include elsewhere. In some cases this may be because you did not know where to include this income and in other cases it will be because you want to use the losses to reduce (offset) the profits of another type of income.

> **Warning:** Only fill in this section after you have completed the supplementary pages for income from employment, self-employment, share schemes, etc. If you don't, you could find that the information should have been included elsewhere on your Tax Return.

Boxes 13.1 to 13.3:

	Amount after tax deducted	Tax deducted	Amount before tax
• Other income	13.1 £	13.2 £	13.3 £

Although casual work is normally classed as employment, if you received a one-off payment for freelance or consultancy work or a commission it may not be classed as income from employment. If that is the case, you can include it here. Profits from isolated literary or artistic activities could be included under self-employment, but if they are not, include them here. If your income counts as a 'trade' you will have to include the figures on the Self-employment, Land and Property or Partnership pages.

Read the list on page 16 of your Inland Revenue notes to check for any items you may have missed and look through your bank statements to see if you have forgotten to include any other items of income. Remember, if you fail to declare some income and the Inland Revenue finds out (either from an employer or even from an informer) you could face penalties.

The following should be included in 'other income':

- *Permanent health insurance* is an insurance that pays out should you be too ill to work. You **only** have to include payments from insurance policies taken out by a **former** employer and if you contributed to the premiums a proportion (equal to the proportion you paid) will be exempt. If you took out your own policy this is **not** taxable. If you received sickness or disability payments from an employer these must be included in the Employment pages.
- *Cashbacks* or *incentive payments* should also be taxed although few realize this. If you receive cash, a car, holiday or had a personal liability waived (for instance a loan written off) as an incentive to buy something (such as a car) or take out a mortgage, you may be taxed on it. Generally, if the cashback is a one-off payment it should escape Income Tax. If you are worried ask the company or person who gave you the incentive.
- Income you received from a business you are no longer involved in (although you can opt to have this taxed as income of the year in which the business ceased by using box **22.5**). This is known as *post cessation income*. It can include recovered bad debts and royalties. Again you can deduct expenses before filling in box **13.3.** See page 17 of your Tax Return Guide for more information. If the income is purely from a change in the way the profits of a business are calculated, you should ask your Tax Office which expenses you can deduct before filling in box **13.3.**
- Accrued income securities such as *interest-bearing securities* including those you can buy to invest in building societies at an above average fixed rate of interest (these are known as *permanent interest-bearing shares* or *PIBS*). Also include government loan stock (but not gilts) and company loan stock. No tax is payable if the nominal value of all accrued income securities held in the tax year did not exceed £5000. However, you should still fill in the box. Shares and other interest received have already been dealt with in ***Q10***. Only include those which had an interest payment between 6 April 1997 and 5 April 1998. This applies even when you sold these securities but the next interest due fell in this period. See page 17 of your Inland Revenue guidance notes for more information and Help Sheet IR325.

If you have more than one type of 'other income' you must add up the total amount. An explanation on the 'Additional information' page may save the Tax Office having to contact you. Ask for Help Sheet *IR325: Other income* which has a copy of a working sheet.

Only fill in box **13.2** if tax was deducted from your income.

> **Tax tip:** Do not forget to deduct capital allowances and expenses incurred in earning any income. The Self-employment pages detail the types of expenses you can deduct and how to claim capital allowances if you bought any items of equipment to help you earn the extra income. You only have to include the amount you make as a profit in box **13.3** – so deduct any expenses before filling in this box. Expenses must be spent solely to earn the income and cannot be spent on things you intend to keep for a while – these need to be deducted as a capital allowance. Ask your Tax Office or tax adviser if you can deduct capital allowances.

Write the total amount of other income you received – or were entitled to receive whether or not it was paid to you – in box **13.3**. If after deducting any expenses you made a loss, enter '0' in box **13.3** and fill in the loss in box **13.6.**

Total up any tax that was deducted in box **13.2**, and the amount paid to you after tax was deducted in box **13.1**. If no tax was deducted leave the tax box blank.

> **Tax tip:** If you invest in PIBS, corporate bonds or government loan stock, the rate of return can be high and you can avoid tax by ensuring that the total value of all accrued interest income securities held at any time is £5000 or less.

Losses brought forward

13.4 £

Losses used in 1997-98

13.5 £

Losses sustained in 1997-98

13.6 £

You can use *losses* (where the amount you have earned does not cover your expenses) to reduce the tax on the same type of income in either this year or future years. In some cases losses can be used to reduce the tax on other types of income. If you have filled in the Self-employment pages you will already know that you can use losses made in your business to reduce the amount of tax you pay on your employment or savings income. The same applies to items you list under 'other income'. For instance, you can offset debts from a business you no longer run against one-off freelance earnings.

But not all types of losses can be offset against other income. See IR 325 for a working sheet of what can and cannot be offset.

If you do not use up your losses this year you can use them to reduce your tax in future years. This is known as *carrying forward*. Then the next year you bring them forward.

Losses included in the other income section can be used to reduce the tax on:

- casual earnings
- one-off freelance income (but not regular work)
- rare literary earnings (articles or poems being published)
- isolated artistic earnings
- sale of patent rights

and a few less common types of earnings.

If you include other income and want to use losses to reduce the tax on this, ask for form IR325.

If you made losses in past years and did not have enough profits to offset these against (and you specified that you wanted to carry or bring forward these losses) write the figure in box **13.4.**

Write in box **13.5** the amount of these previous years' losses you are offsetting in 1997/98. If your losses are less than your 1997/98 profits in box **13.3** you must use up the whole amount. However, you can only do this if you are allowed to offset these losses against the type of income included in box **13.3.** So if your previous losses were for isolated artistic earnings you will not be able to offset these against permanent health insurance payments included in this section of your tax return.

Note: You cannot set losses against annual payments from unit trusts or from former employers.

In box **13.6** enter the total amount of your losses. Losses you cannot use this year and you want to carry forward to offset against future profits from similar income should be recorded on IR 325.

Do not include losses from a discontinued business, called *post cessation losses* – these go in box **15.11.**

8

TAX RELIEF ON PENSIONS, MORTGAGES, CHARITABLE GIVING AND OTHER LOANS AND INVESTMENTS

Tax relief reduces your tax bill by giving you tax back or reducing the amount of tax you have to pay. In most cases you get tax relief at the top rate of tax you pay although some reliefs such as MIRAS (mortgage interest tax relief) are *restricted* to 10 per cent.

Some tax relief is given *at source*, which means you do not have to claim it and get it automatically even if you are non-taxpayer.

However, in other cases even when tax relief is given at source – for instance on personal pension contributions – if you want to claim higher-rate tax relief you may have to ask for it.

You can only claim higher-rate tax relief if you pay higher rate (40 per cent) tax. You get tax relief by a reduction in the amount of income that would be taxed at 40 per cent.

This chapter deals with tax relief for:

- pension contributions including additional voluntary contributions;
- vocational training payments;
- interest on qualifying loans including mortgages;
- maintenance payments;
- investments in venture capital trusts or Enterprise Investment schemes;
- payments to charities;
- payments to trade unions or friendly societies for death benefits;
- costs incurred after the close of a business (post-cessation expenses);
- losses on relevant discounted securities.

Note: Mortgages that are part of MIRAS (mortgage interest relief at source) do not have to be included on your Tax Return as mortgage relief is given automatically.

Q14: Pension contributions

PAPERWORK REQUIRED

- ❑ Details of any contributions to personal pension plans or retirement annuity contracts if you are self-employed, in partnership or an employee.
- ❑ Details of payments to free-standing top-up pension schemes (FSAVCs) if you were an employee.

This section does **not** include company or occupational pension schemes as any pension contributions deducted from your pay receive tax relief automatically. So if you are in a company scheme tick the ***NO*** box unless:

- ❑ you paid into a top-up pension scheme not linked to your company pension, known as free-standing additional voluntary contributions (FSAVCs); and/or
- ❑ any employee contributions to a company scheme were **not** deducted at source from pay.

In these two cases tick the ***YES*** box.

This section covers:

- ❑ personal pensions taken out by employees who are not in company pension schemes;
- ❑ personal pension schemes (and old-style personal pensions known as *retirement annuity contracts*) taken out by the self-employed.

If you have one of these pensions tick the ***YES*** box.

You get tax relief at your highest rate on contributions to personal pension plans. So for every £1 you invest you get 40p in tax relief if you are a higher-rate taxpayer.

There are limits on the contributions you can pay for each year. You cannot pay more than a set percentage of your *net relevant earnings*.

This will be your pay plus bonuses if you are employed minus any expenses or payroll donations to charity. If you are **self-employed** or in **partnership** the net relevant earnings are your taxable business profits (your turnover minus your expenses figure in box **3.89**) or your share of the partnership profits (box **4.19)**, or if you have profits from furnished holiday lettings, the profit in box **5.14**.

With personal pensions you can only pay contributions on net relevant earnings up to the £84,000 *earnings cap* in the 1997/98 tax year (rising to £87,600 in 1998/99). This earnings cap usually increases at the start of a new tax year. However, there is no earnings cap on retirement annuities.

Tables 8.1 and 8.2 give the maximum contributions you can make to a personal pension or retirement annuity plan. The amount you can contribute rises with age (at the end of the tax year).

Table 8.1 *How much you can pay into a personal pension (contribution limits as a percentage of net relevant earnings)*

Age on 6 April	% of pay	maximum contribution
35 or less	17.5%	£14,700
36–45	20%	£16,800
46–50	25%	£21,000
51–55	30%	£25,200
56–60	35%	£29,400
61 or over	40%	£33,600

Table 8.2 *How much you can pay into a retirement annuity plan (These are pre 1 July 1988 personal pension plans with no earnings cap)*

Age on 6 April	% of pay
50 or less	17.5%
51–55	20%
56–60	22.5%
61 or over	27.5%

Tax tips:

- You can also pay 5 per cent of these contributions into a life insurance policy which pays out on death before 75. You can therefore get tax relief on life insurance contributions.

- Because there is no earnings cap on retirement annuities, higher earners who have existing (pre-1 July 1988) plans may find these better than personal pension plans even though the maximum contribution limits are lower.
- If you have an old-style retirement annuity and your salary is within the earnings cap (less than £87,600) and likely to remain so, consider taking out a personal pension scheme as the contribution limits are higher. Although you can have both a retirement annuity and a personal pension, you cannot get maximum tax relief on both. Ask for Help Sheet *IR330: Pension payments* for further information.

Tax warning: If you are lucky enough to have an employer who contributes to your personal pension plan, remember that the maximum contribution limits **include** employer contributions and **no** tax relief is given on employer's contributions.

HOW TAX RELIEF IS GIVEN

You can only make contributions to personal pension plans out of *net relevant earnings*, which means you can only pay pension contributions out of:

- any earnings from non-pensionable employment;
- profits from self-employment;
- your share of partnership profits;
- profits from furnished holiday lettings.

You cannot make contributions out of savings income.

If you are self-employed your pension contributions will reduce the level of your profits which are liable to tax. So if you pay in £10,000 of contributions, £10,000 of your profits will no longer be taxed. If you are a higher-rate taxpayer you will therefore save £4000 of tax. Your relief will be limited to a percentage of your *net relevant earnings* (see Table 8.2).

If you are an employee paying into a personal pension, basic-rate tax relief of 23 per cent will automatically be invested in your pension because you pay your contributions *net* of tax relief.

For instance, if you pay in £77 a month, £23 a month will be paid in by the Inland Revenue. If you contribute £100 a month this rises to £130 following tax relief. Any higher-rate tax relief will be calculated using your Tax Return and you will get a tax rebate and/or your Tax Code will be adjusted so that you receive higher-rate tax relief through your PAYE earnings. Even if you do **not** want to claim higher rate relief you must **still** include pension contributions on your Tax Return.

If you are an employee paying into a retirement annuity, no tax relief is given when you make the contributions as you pay them *gross*. Tax relief is usually given through your PAYE Code.

HOW TO MAXIMIZE TAX RELIEF

If you have *net relevant earnings* in any year but do not pay the maximum permitted contributions, the difference between what you actually contribute and what you could have paid is *unused tax relief*. This tax relief can be carried forward so you can use up this extra tax relief in future years. You can *carry forward* the unused allowance for the next six tax years. The unused relief will be in addition to the maximum relief for that year. Ask for Help Sheet *IR330: Pension payments.*

> **Tax tip:** If you are **not** earning enough to pay 40 per cent tax, but think you will next year or in future years, consider carrying forward some or all of your unused relief to a year when you can get tax relief at 40 per cent instead of 23 per cent.

You can also *carry back* pension contributions to get tax relief for a past tax year. You can only carry back premiums to the preceding tax year. But if you had **no** *net relevant earnings* in that year, you can carry back to the year before that. You can do this either using your tax return or by making a separate election to your Tax Office by 31 January 1999. Ask for form PP43 (or 43 if you have a retirement annuity).

> **Tax tip:** If you are a basic rate taxpayer this year but were a higher 40 per cent taxpayer last year and did not make maximum contributions last year, consider carrying back premiums so you can get tax relief at the higher rate.

You can also *bring back* contributions made after 5 April 1998 but before you send in your Tax Return. So if you make a pension contribution in June 1998 you can include it on your Tax Return for tax year to 5 April 1998 (the one you are now filling in) and claim tax relief a year earlier. If you have sent in your Tax Return before making the post-5 April 1998 contributions, you can make an election before waiting for your 5 April 1999 Tax Return.

If you want to carry back, carry forward or bring back payments or you have exceeded the appropriate percentage limits of your earnings, ask for Help Sheet IR330. Doctors and dentists should ask for leaflet IR1 from the Orderline.

Personal pension plans taken out before 1 July 1988 are called retirement annuity contracts. If you pay into both a retirement annuity contract and personal pension plan there are special rules. Ask for Help Sheet IR330.

> **Tax warning:** If you have paid in more than the percentage of earnings allowed, ask for Help Sheet *IR330: Pension payments.*

RETIREMENT ANNUITIES AND SELF-EMPLOYED PENSION CONTRIBUTIONS

Q14 **Do you want to claim relief for pension contributions?** NO [ ] YES [ ] If yes, fill in boxes 14.1 to 14.17 as appropriate.

*Do not include contributions deducted from your pay by your employer to their pension scheme, because tax relief is given automatically. But **do include** your contributions to personal pension schemes.*

■ ***Retirement annuity contracts***

Qualifying payments made in 1997-98	14.1 £	1997-98 payments used in an earlier year	14.2 £
1997-98 payments now to be carried back	14.3 £	Payments brought back from 1998-99	14.4 £

Relief claimed: box 14.1 *minus* (boxes 14.2 and 14.3, but not 14.4) 14.5 £

■ ***Self-employed contributions to personal pension plans***

Qualifying payments made in 1997-98	14.6 £	1997-98 payments used in an earlier year	14.7 £
1997-98 payments now to be carried back	14.8 £	Payments brought back from 1998-99	14.9 £

Relief claimed: box 14.6 *minus* (boxes 14.7 and 14.8, but not 14.9) 14.10 £

Note: Retirement annuity contracts are those taken out pre-1 July 1988. Personal pensions are contracts taken out after this date. The retirement annuity boxes should be filled in by employees with pre-1988 retirement annuities.

Boxes 14.1 and 14.6:

Enter the total contributions for the year.

Boxes 14.2 and 14.7:

If you made payments in the 1997/98 tax year but included these payments on a previous Tax Return (you carried them back to the last tax year and asked for this on your 1996/97 Tax Return) write in the amount here. The same applies if you have written to your Tax Office and asked for an election for payments to be carried back.

Boxes 14.3 and 14.8:

These are contributions you want to carry back to earlier years. As explained above, if you did not pay in the maximum allowed last year you can *carry back* a contribution made this year either to get higher-rate tax relief from a past year or so that you can pay in more than the maximum allowed this year.

Boxes 14.4 and 14.9:

This is for contributions made after the end of the tax year (after 5 April 1998) which you want to be classed as contributions for the tax year ending 5 April 1998.

Boxes 14.5 and 14.10:

Follow the simple sum on your Tax Return to arrive at the amount of relief you want to claim.

Tax tip: If you realize you are going to face a large tax bill for 1997/98 (the one covered by your Tax Return) and want to reduce it after the end of the tax year, you can do this by making a pension contribution after 5 April but before you send in your Tax Return. Put the amount in the boxes **14.4**, **14.9** or **14.14**. Remember you can only do this if you did not contribute the maximum percentage of your net relevant earnings into a pension in the 1997/98 tax year.

EMPLOYEES WHO ARE NOT MEMBERS OF COMPANY PENSION SCHEMES

■ ***Employee contributions to personal pension plans*** *(include your gross contribution - see the note on box 14.11 in your Tax Return Guide)*

Qualifying payments made in 1997-98	14.11 £	1997-98 payments used in an earlier year	14.12 £	Relief claimed
1997-98 payments now to be carried back	14.13 £	Payments brought back from 1998-99	14.14 £	box 14.11 *minus* (boxes 14.12 and 14.13, but not 14.14) 14.15 £

Box 14.11:

Enter the *gross* amounts (before tax is deducted). For employees this figure has to be calculated as you pay in a *net* amount and then basic-rate tax relief is paid in by the Inland Revenue. So, you have already received 23 per cent tax relief. To work out the gross figure, divide the amount you paid into your plan by 77 and multiply the answer by 100.

So if you paid in £100 a month, your gross figure will be:

£100 x 12 (months) = £1200 (net annual amount)/
£1200 ÷ 77 x 100 = £1558 (gross annual amount)

Boxes 14.12, 14.13 and 14.14:

These are contributions you want to carry back to earlier years. Follow the instructions for boxes **14.2**, **14.3** and **14.4**. Again, don't forget to write in the gross amount.

Box 14.15:

Follow the simple calculation instructions on your Tax Return to arrive at this figure.

EMPLOYEES WHO *ARE* MEMBERS OF COMPANY SCHEMES

• Amount of contributions to employer's schemes **not deducted** at source from pay 14.16 £

Box 14.16:

This box will not affect many people, only those whose contributions to their employer's scheme were **not** deducted at source from pay. In most cases employees' contributions to company schemes are automatically deducted from your salary before the amount of tax you pay is calculated. This means you do not pay any tax on the contributions made to the scheme and, as such, you effectively receive tax relief at source on this proportion of your pay because no tax is payable on this amount. Do **not** include payment contributions deducted from your pay by your employer. Only include any lump-sum additional voluntary contributions which did not get tax relief at source.

Doctors and dentists whose NHS earnings are classed as self-employed profits should read the notes on page 20 of the Tax Return Guide.

Box 14.17:

- Gross amount of free-standing additional voluntary contributions paid in 1997-98 **14.17** £

Free-standing additional voluntary contributions (FSAVCs) are top-up pension schemes that are **not** linked to company pension schemes but taken out by members of company pension schemes to boost the amount of pension they will receive. The top-up schemes offered by your company pension scheme are known as AVCs (they enable you to increase the amount of contributions normally paid into your company scheme). Do **not** include AVCs in this box.

You must enter the total *gross* amount of contributions during the tax year.

Again, to calculate the *gross* amount you will have to add back the 23 per cent tax relief you are automatically given. Divide your contributions by 77 and multiply that figure by 100 to give the gross amount.

The total amount of contributions must still not exceed the overall limits. As an employee you can only pay 15 per cent of your earnings up to £84,000 into **all** pension plans including your company pension scheme, additional voluntary contribution plan (AVCs) and free-standing additional voluntary contribution schemes (FSAVCs).

Q15: Other tax reliefs

PAPERWORK REQUIRED

- ❑ Details of any vocational training costs you have incurred (NVQ or SVQ).
- ❑ Details of any mortgages **not** in MIRAS. You should have a certificate of loan interest paid from your lender.
- ❑ Interest payments on loans secured on your home to buy a life annuity if you are over 65 and this is **not** linked to a pension. These are also known as home income plans.
- ❑ Interest details if you took out a loan to buy shares or fund a small company or partnership.
- ❑ Documentation covering all maintenance and alimony payments.
- ❑ Subscriptions to venture capital trusts or enterprise investment schemes.
- ❑ Amounts you have given to charities under Gift Aid or covenant.
- ❑ Details of any expenses incurred in a business that has ceased (post-cessation expenses).
- ❑ Losses incurred on investing in any relevant discounted securities (deep discount bonds).
- ❑ Payments made to a trade union or friendly society for death benefits.

Read page 20 of your Tax Return Guide which explains these reliefs and what you can claim.

Box 15.1:

- Payments you made for vocational training

Amount of payment
15.1 £

Tax relief is given to those who pay for their own vocational training provided this counts towards a National or Scottish Vocational Qualification. So even if you are only doing one of the five levels or 'units of competence' and are not studying for the full qualification, you can still get tax relief. However, any payments for GCSEs or A-level courses do **not** qualify for tax relief even when they are taken as a preliminary course to an NVQ or SVQ.

Tax tip: You can also get tax relief for training which does not involve NVQs or SVQs if it provides skills or knowledge which are relevant to – and intended to be used in – paid employment or self-employment. To qualify, the course must be full time for at least four consecutive weeks but for no more than a year, and you must be aged 30 or over.

To qualify, you must be:

- ❑ aged 16, 17 or 18 but not in full-time education at a school; or
- ❑ aged 19 or over and paying for your own training; and
- ❑ not in receipt of any grants or assistance under a government scheme.

You will usually know if the scheme qualifies for tax relief as basic-rate tax relief is deducted from your fees before you pay them. So if the training costs are £400, you pay them after basic-rate tax is deducted. So you pay £400 – 23 per cent (£92) = £308. You save the basic-rate tax of £92 and this is your tax relief. Write the figure after tax relief in box **15.1.**

If you are a higher rate taxpayer you can claim the further tax relief of 17 per cent (40 per cent – 23 per cent = 17 per cent) by filling in box **15.1**. Ask for leaflet *IR119: Tax relief for vocation training* before filling in this box.

Box 15.2: mortgage interest

	Amount of payment
• Interest on loans to buy your main home (other than MIRAS)	15.2 £

Mortgage interest relief on loans to buy your main home rarely has to be claimed as it is given automatically by most lenders under the MIRAS scheme with tax relief deducted from your mortgage payments. Relief is 15 per cent of the interest payments on the first £30,000 of a home loan used to buy your only or main home. This was reduced to 10 per cent from April 1998.

However, if your mortgage is **not** covered by MIRAS you **must** claim tax relief.

To work out the figure to write in box **15.2** ask for Help Sheet *IR340: Relief on loans not in MIRAS* and work through the sheet to get the amount you want to claim.

If you get a *free or low-interest mortgage from your employer* you can also claim tax relief on any taxable benefit. This is explained in Part 3, Chapter 11 on employee benefits and expenses. Ask for leaflet *IR145: Low-interest loans provided by employers.*

Tax tips:

- ❑ If you took out a loan to pay for home improvements before 6 April 1988 it would have qualified for tax relief (provided that when it was added to your other loans you came within the MIRAS threshold). This tax relief was scrapped on home improvement loans taken out after that date. So if you have a pre-6 April 1988 loan, think twice about repaying it or switching it to a cheaper loan. If you do, you will lose the tax relief.
- ❑ Mortgage interest relief is equally split on joint mortgages taken out by married couples. But if one partner is a non-taxpayer and your mortgage is **not** in MIRAS you could be wasting this relief. Elect to have the entire or bulk of the mortgage tax relief given to the partner who is a taxpayer. Remember this is only for loans that are not in MIRAS. You should fill in Form 15 and have a year from the end of the tax year in which to make the change.
- ❑ If you marry, each partner can continue to receive £30,000 tax relief on their individual properties for up to 12 months after the wedding **and** can also qualify for a further £30,000 of tax relief on a mortgage to buy a new marital home. This means that newly weds can get MIRAS on £90,000 of home loans – but for up to one year only.
- ❑ If you are moving home and have not been able to sell your existing property you can receive tax relief on both properties for up to one year. This tax relief is also available on bridging loans.
- ❑ If you expect to become a non-taxpayer in the future make sure your loan is in MIRAS as you will still qualify for tax relief even though you do not pay tax. If the loan is not in MIRAS you will have to make a separate claim for relief.
- ❑ Mortgage tax relief is not restricted to houses and flats, it can also apply to caravans and houseboats if these are your only or main home.
- ❑ If you took out a mortgage with another person before 1 August 1998 (and still have the same home loan) each buyer will qualify for £30,000 of tax relief. So if two of you bought the property you would have £60,000 of tax relief between you. Think twice before switching your loan as you will lose and will come under new rules which restrict mortgage tax relief to £30,000 per property instead of £30,000 per home buyer. The same applies if you marry but bought your home, with your partner, before 1 August 1998 – your tax relief will be halved when you wed.

- ❑ If you use part of your home for business you can treat the loan to buy your property as two separate loans and claim mortgage interest relief for the proportion relating to the residential use of the property but no mortgage interest relief on the part relating to business use. However, you can deduct the interest on the business proportion of the loan against your business profits. You must split the loan in proportion to the amount of the property used for business. Ask your Tax Office for advice.
- ❑ If you let more than a third of your home you should opt out of MIRAS although you may still be able to claim tax relief directly and save even more tax. If you opt out you can claim a proportion of your mortgage interest (or all of the interest if your entire property is let) to reduce your rental profits and therefore tax. And instead of tax relief being restricted to 15 per cent of the first £30,000 you will save tax at the highest rate of tax you pay on all the allowable interest regardless of the size of the loan.

Box 15.3: Tax relief on other loans

	Amount of payment
• Interest on other qualifying loans	15.3 £

The qualifying loans included in this box are as follows:

- ❑ Loans you take out to lend money to or buy shares in a company in which you either own 5 per cent of the share capital or own part of the share capital and are also an employee. These cover *close companies* and *employee controlled companies*.
- ❑ Loans to buy an interest in a trading or professional *partnership* or to buy plant or machinery for that partnership or to provide that partnership with capital **provided** your interest costs have not been included in the partnership accounts or on the partnership pages. Normally the interest payments are deducted from your profits before calculating tax. Loans for self-employment should already be included on the relevant pages, as should loans to buy a property for let.
- ❑ Loans to buy shares in or lend money to a business co-operative.
- ❑ Loans to buy plant or machinery for use in your work for your employer.

You get tax relief on these loans at your top rate of tax.

Box **15.3** also covers interest on loans to buy *life annuities* for the over 65s, which are also known as *home income plans.* The loan must be secured on your only or main home and the borrower or person who receives the annuity must be 65 or over when the loan is made.

These schemes are a way for the elderly to receive an income from the cash tied up in their property. They take out a loan secured on their home and buy an annuity which then covers the interest payments on the loan and gives them a regular income.

Tax relief is given at the **basic rate of tax**, 23 per cent, and is **not** restricted to 15 per cent like mortgage tax relief.

If you have one of these plans ask for Help Sheet *IR340: Relief for loans not in MIRAS*.

> **Tax tip:** You may also be able to claim relief for any low-interest or interest-free loans from your employer if you have been taxed on these as an employee benefit. Ask for *IR145: Low-interest loans provided by employers.*

Boxes 15.4, 15.5 and 15.6: Maintenance or alimony payments

- Maintenance or alimony payments you have made under a court order, Child Support Agency assessment or legally binding order or agreement

Amount claimed under 'new' rules
15.4 £

Amount claimed under 'old' rules up to £1,830
15.5 £

Amount claimed under 'old' rules over £1,830
15.6 £

Tax relief is given on payments to a spouse or former spouse or child following divorce or under a verbal or written separation agreement, court order or Child Support Agency assessment.

You **cannot** get tax relief for other payments including voluntary payments or payments made to your children if they are aged 21 or over.

You cannot claim the maintenance tax relief on lump sums as part of a divorce settlement even if these are paid in instalments. And if you pay your former spouse's mortgage and get mortgage tax relief you cannot claim tax relief again. Any other bills covered by the court order or legal agreement count towards the £1830 limit, rising to £1900 from April 1998.

Tax relief varies depending on whether you have an *existing obligation* covered by the 'old rules' or not.

The 'old rules' apply if:

- ❑ maintenance payments were agreed or made by court order **before 15 March 1988**, or a court order made by 30 June 1988 which was applied for on or before 15 March 1988; or
- ❑ if you make maintenance payments under a written agreement or deed which was made before 15 March 1988 or submitted to your Inspector of Taxes by 30 June 1988.

If the 'old rules' apply you fill in box **15.5**. But do not simply write in the amount of maintenance you paid. You must first compare the amount of maintenance you paid in the April 1997 to April 1998 tax year with the amount on which you received tax relief in the 1988 to 1989 tax year. You must use the **smaller** of these two figures.

So if you paid £2000 maintenance in 1997/98 and £1800 maintenance in 1988/89, the figure you must write in box **15.5** will be £1800.

However, the tax relief is restricted to the first £1830 of payments and the rate of relief is 15 per cent.

So if you paid £3000 of maintenance in both 1997/98 and in 1988/89, the figure you must write in box **15.5** will be £1830. The figure will either be £1830 or the amount you paid in maintenance (the smaller of the 1997/98 and 1988/89 figures), whichever is the lower.

Any maintenance payments above this £1830 threshold qualify for tax relief at your highest rate of tax by reducing the amount of income taxed at that rate. So, to follow the example above, in box **15.6** you should write £3000 – £1830 = £1170.

You can get tax relief if you pay maintenance directly to a child, but you only get tax relief on the amount of maintenance you paid which qualified for tax relief in 1988/89.

If you have to pay maintenance payments to more than one former spouse you can get tax relief on both under the 'old rules'. This is the sum of the lower of the two amounts (either the 1998/89 figure or the 1997/98 amount) for each agreement.

If the court order CSA assessment or agreement, was made on or after **15 March 1988** 'new rules' apply and you can only get tax relief up to the £1830 limit with this relief restricted to 15 per cent (falling to 10 per cent from April 1998). There is no additional tax relief unlike under the old rules.

So in box **15.4** you must write either £1830 or the amount of maintenance you paid if this is lower.

If you make two lots of maintenance payments, one under the 'old rules' and one under the 'new rules', you can get tax relief under both sets of rules. The tax relief under the 'new rules' is only given if the figure in box **15.5** is less than £1830. Subtract the figure in box **15.5** from £1830 and enter in box **15.4** the lower of:

- that figure; or
- the amount you paid in 1997/98 under your 'new rules' arrangement.

Tax tips:

- If you paid more in maintenance in 1997/98 than in 1988/89 you may be better off electing for the 'new rules' to apply, but only if you currently pay less than £1830 a year in maintenance. By switching you can claim tax relief on the higher amount of maintenance. This is because any increases in your maintenance payments are not taken into account under the 'old rules'. You must make the election within 12 months of the end of the tax year and write to inform the person to whom you pay maintenance. Once you have switched to the new system you cannot change back.
- Do not elect to switch from the 'old rules' if you make payments directly to a child as they do not qualify for tax relief under the 'new rules'.
- If your maintenance payments are above £1830 – and were above this in 1988/89 – you will be better off under the 'old rules' so be careful not to change any arrangement as the new rules will apply.
- You cannot get tax relief for payments made directly to a child under the 'new rules' so ensure that any agreements specify that payments are made to your former spouse.
- Any voluntary maintenance payments you make do not qualify for tax relief. Only enforceable maintenance arrangements made under a court order, a legally-binding written agreement or under an assessment by the Child Support Agency qualify for tax relief. So ensure you have a legal agreement.
- Only if the spouse has not remarried (or is unlikely to) will you be better off under the 'new rules' as once your former spouse remarries you lose all tax relief. So if your former spouse is likely to remarry, do not switch to the 'new rules'.

Note: Tax relief can either be given through your PAYE tax code or a lower tax bill/tax rebate by filling in a Tax Return or informing your Tax Office.

Important: You must give information including dates and details of the type of agreement or court order in the 'Additional information' box on page 8 of your Tax Return.

For more information ask for *IR93: Separation, divorce and maintenance payments.*

Boxes 15.7 and 15.8: Venture Capital Trusts and Enterprise Investment Schemes

	Amount on which relief claimed
• Subscriptions for Venture Capital Trust shares (up to £100,000)	15.7 £
• Subscriptions under the Enterprise Investment Scheme (up to £100,000)	15.8 £

These offer tax breaks **when you invest** so they are a good way to reduce your tax bill quickly. However, the risks can be high. Tax relief of 20 per cent is given on investments up to £100,000, giving a maximum tax relief of £20,000.

Venture capital trusts are funds which in turn invest in growing business. You must hold the shares for a minimum of five years. Any dividends paid out by the trust or gains you make when you sell the shares in the trust are also tax free. Enterprise Investment Schemes also encourage investment in small unquoted companies.

Tax warning: Both of these schemes are currently under review and, as such, may not exist or may not offer the same tax breaks in future.

If you have invested in an enterprise investment scheme you **must** have either form EIS3 or EIS5 to fill in this section. Do not fill in this box until you receive the form. You must also include any investments during the tax year for which you have already received relief in your Tax Code (your PAYE tax has been altered to give you tax relief already).

You must write details of each EIS investment in the 'Additional information' box on page 8 of your Tax Return.

Boxes 15.9 and 15.10: Charitable payments

		Amount of payment
• Charitable covenants or annuities	15.9	£
		Amount of payment
• Gift Aid	15.10	£

Two types of charitable payments qualify for tax relief. Charitable covenants are legally binding agreements to pay a certain amount to charity for more than three years. Gift Aid donations must be at least £250 and made in cash.

Both are ways for you to give to charity in a tax-efficient manner. In both cases basic tax relief of 23 per cent is given automatically as the charity can recover this from the Inland Revenue.

So for every £77 you pay in, the charity reclaims £23 tax relief. Or if you pay in £100, the charity can claim £30, bringing the total donation up to £130.

However, if you are a higher rate taxpayer **you**, not the charity, claim the higher-rate tax relief. The extra tax relief is the difference between the higher rate and basic rate of tax (40 per cent − 23 per cent = 17 per cent). You claim this higher-rate relief on your Tax Return. So as a higher-rate taxpayer, on a £100 donation you will get 17 per cent tax relief = £17.

Although basic tax relief is claimed by the charity, do **not** gross up the amounts paid to take this into account. Simply add up the total payments made during the tax year.

Box 15.11: Post-cessation expenses

		Amount of payment
• Post-cessation expenses and losses on relevant discounted securities etc.	15.11	£

This box is for those who used to run a business and incurred expenses related to that business after it ceased.

As this book is primarily aimed at employees rather than the self-employed, it does not look in detail at this subject. In summary, if you have to pay out for remedying faulty goods or pay any damages for

Tax tips:

- ❑ Even if you are not a higher-rate taxpayer (and as such cannot claim tax relief on your charitable donations) consider making all charity payments either through covenants or Gift Aid as the charity can then receive more by claiming basic-rate tax on what you donate.
- ❑ Using a covenant to give to charity can have its benefits. For instance, if you donate to the National Trust or another charitable body you may receive free or reduced-priced entry to the charity's properties.
- ❑ If you are married and want to make charitable donations through a covenant or Gift Aid, make sure that the partner who is the higher-rate taxpayer makes the payment – that way you can claim higher-rate tax relief.

faulty work or services, you can offset these costs within seven years of the business ceasing. You can also claim back tax relief on any bad debts which were not deducted from profits. See page 22 of the Tax Return Guide for further information.

Deep discounted securities include gilt strips. Losses can only be offset against other income in the same tax year.

Box 15.12: Trade union and friendly society payments for death benefits

	Half amount of payment
• Payments to a trade union or friendly society for death benefits	**15.12** £

This is a tax relief that few people know about. You can claim tax relief for:

- ❑ the part of your trade union subscription that pays for a pension (superannuation), life assurance or funeral benefits;
- ❑ the part of any friendly society premiums paid to provide sickness and death benefits provided the premium is **no** more than £25 per month **and** 40 per cent or less of the premiums is charged for the death benefit.

But you do not get tax relief on all of the amount. Find out from your trade union or friendly society how much of your premium provides the pension, life assurance, funeral or death benefit. Then divide this amount by **half** and write this figure in box **15.12**. This is because tax relief is only given on one half of the amount you pay.

Tax tips:

- ❑ If you have an option to pay for life insurance or death benefits through a trade union or friendly society, take the offer up as this is one of the only ways you can get tax relief on your payments. The other is buying life insurance through your pension.
- ❑ Always check with your trade union or friendly society to see if tax relief is available as you may be unaware that you can claim this relief.

9

TAX ALLOWANCES

Tax allowances are explained in greater detail in Chapter 3 of this book, which you should read to understand how allowances, allowance restrictions and earnings restrictions affect your tax bill. **It is important you understand how allowances work as they are one of the easiest ways to reduce your tax bill**.

PAPERWORK REQUIRED

- ❑ PAYE Coding notices (if you have received these) telling you what allowances you are already claiming/receiving.
- ❑ Details of any registration with a local authority if you are registered blind.
- ❑ Marriage details (dates).
- ❑ Any correspondence from the Inland Revenue about tax allowances.

Tax tip: Even if you have forgotten to claim a tax allowance for a previous tax year, you can still make a tax saving. This is because you can go back six years to claim an allowance you did not know you were entitled to. Tax relief will be given at the rate of tax which would have applied at that time.

Q16: Allowances

It is important that you read through all the questions before ticking the ***YES*** or ***NO*** box at the top of page 6.

Q16 ***You get your personal allowance of £4,045 automatically. If you were born before 6 April 1933, enter your date of birth in box 21.4** - you may get higher age-related allowances.*

Do you want to claim any of the following allowances? NO ☐ YES ☐ If yes, please read pages 23 to 26 of your Tax Return Guide and then fill in boxes 16.1 to 16.28 as appropriate.

You should only tick the ***NO*** box if:

- ❑ you are not married and were not married during the tax year;
- ❑ you are not a single parent/do not have a dependent child living with you;
- ❑ you were not widowed during the tax year or the year earlier;
- ❑ you are not registered blind;
- ❑ you have not been receiving the transitional allowance for married women with husbands on low income; and
- ❑ you do not want to transfer surplus allowances to your spouse (see the section on Boxes **16.25** to **16.28** for more details).

Note: Even if you tick the ***NO*** box you should still read the Tax Tips at the end of this section as you may find that you can claim an allowance for a previous year or in a future year.

Please note that you do ***not*** have to claim the basic personal allowance. This is the allowance automatically given to everyone (apart from non-residents). The allowance for the 1997/98 tax year (the one covered by your Tax Return) is £4045. The allowance means that you do **not** pay tax on the first £4045 of income you earn.

Special rules for those aged 65 or over

The personal allowance rises with age. Those aged 65 or over during the tax year get an increased personal allowance of £5220 and those aged 75 or over an increased age allowance of £5400. As with the personal allowance, you do **not** need to claim these age-related allowances. The married couple's allowance also rises with age. To qualify for higher age-related allowances you – or your spouse in the case of the married couple's allowance – must have reached 65 or 75 on or before 5 April 1998. However, if your income is £15,600 or more, your allowances will be reduced. See the calculation on page 15 in Part 1 of this book.

Boxes 16.1 and 16.2: Blind person's allowance

	Date of registration (if first year of claim)	Local authority (or other register)
■ *Blind person's allowance*	16.1 / /	16.2

Allowance: £1280

You can only claim this if you are registered blind with a local authority. Write the name of this authority in box **16.2**.

Only fill in box **16.1** if this is your first year of claiming. Note that you can still get the allowance for the year ended 5 April 1998 even if you had not registered as blind provided you already had evidence of blindness at that date (usually an ophthalmologist's certificate).

Note that if you live in Scotland or Northern Ireland you can also claim the allowance if you are not able to perform any work for which eyesight is essential. Write 'Scotland Claim' or 'Northern Ireland claim' in box **16.2** if this is the case.

Boxes 16.3 and 16.4: Transitional allowance

- Tick to claim and give details in the 'Additional information' box on page 8 *(please see page 23 of your Tax Return Guide for what is needed)* 16.3
- If you want to calculate your tax, enter the amount of transitional allowance you can have in box 16.4 16.4 £

Allowance: It is generally the personal allowance of £4045 less your husband's income for the tax year ending 5 April 1998. So if his income is £2000, your transitional allowance will be £2045.

This can only be claimed by married women who were in receipt of the transitional allowance in the 1996/97 tax year.

It is given to some wives with husbands on low income. To meet the requirements they must:

- ❑ still be living with the same husband as in the whole of the 1996/97 tax year;
- ❑ be married to a husband who was resident in the UK during the tax year; and
- ❑ the husband must have written to his Tax Office asking for the allowance to be given to the wife.

To claim, the wife must tick box **16.3** and give details of her husband's name, address, tax reference, National Insurance number and Tax Office in the 'Additional information' box on page 8 of the Tax Return.

Only fill in box **16.4** if you want to calculate your own tax liability. If you do, write in the amount of allowance agreed with your husband or ask your Tax Office for the figure to put in the box.

■ ***Married couple's allowance for a married man*** *- see page 23 of your Tax Return Guide.*

- Wife's full name **16.5**
- Date of marriage (if after 5 April 1997) **16.6** / /
- Wife's date of birth (if before 6 April 1933) **16.7** / /
- Tick box 16.8 if you or your wife have allocated **half** the allowance to her **16.8**
- Wife's tax reference (if known, please) **16.9**
- Tick box 16.10 if you and your wife have allocated **all** the allowance to her **16.10**

Married and separated men: married couple's allowance

Allowance: £1830 (with the amount of tax relief restricted to 15 per cent giving a maximum tax saving of £275). This allowance rises with age to £3185 (also restricted to 15 per cent) if one spouse is aged 65 or over during the tax year and to £3225 (also restricted to 15 per cent tax relief) if one spouse is aged 75 or over during the tax year. This tax allowance rises to £1900 from April 1998).

Only fill these boxes in if you are:

- ❑ a married man (women need to fill in boxes **16.11** to **16.15**); or
- ❑ were a married man during the tax year but are now separated from your wife.

> **Tax tip:** Even if you were separated from your wife before 6 April 1991 **but** you were **still** married to her on 6 April 1997 **and** have wholly maintained her since separation until at least 6 April 1997 with voluntary payments for which you were not entitled to tax relief, you may still be able to claim the married couple's allowance. Ask your Tax Office for advice.

Tax rules state that you must be 'living' with your wife. However, this does not mean you have to live under the same roof, only that you are still married and neither of you intends to make the separation permanent.

Boxes 16.5, 16.7 and 16.9:

Write your wife's full name, her date of birth (if before 6 April 1933 so that you can claim any higher age-related married couple's allowance) and her tax reference number if you have this.

Box 16.6:

Write your date of marriage if it was after 5 April 1997.

Special rules for newly weds

If you married during the tax year (between 6 April 1997 and 5 April 1998) you may not be able to claim the full married couple's allowance. The tax relief is given for every month of marriage during the tax year and is reduced by each complete tax month (from 6th of one month to the 5th of the next) which has passed before the wedding.

So if you marry on 1 July, the complete tax months of April, May and June do not qualify for married couple's allowance, ie three months out of 12, so your allowance of £1830 will be reduced by 3/12 = £1373.

Tax tips:

- ❑ You should **not** claim the married couple's allowance for your new marriage if you were entitled to the full married couple's allowance from a previous marriage. This is because you can claim the married couple's allowance for the whole year – not just for the part of the year in which you remarried. If you do not want to claim the married couple's allowance for your new marriage do **not** fill in box **16.6;** simply fill in the boxes with your previous wife's details.
- ❑ You should **not** claim the married couple's allowance if you are entitled to claim the additional personal allowance because you have a child living with you. This is because you can claim the entire additional personal allowance (which is the same as the married couple's allowance) but can only claim the married couple's allowance from the date you married. Note, you cannot claim the additional personal allowance **and** the married couple's allowance. If you want to claim the additional personal allowance do **not** fill in boxes **16.5** to **16.10**. Fill in boxes **16.16** to **16.23** instead.

Boxes 16.8 and 16.10: Allocating all or half of the allowance to your wife

Your wife can ask for half of the married couple's allowance to be offset against her tax – without your permission. However, she must do this by the start of the relevant tax year – so this cannot be backdated.

If she wants to claim the whole allowance, she needs your permission as this must be a joint election. Again this must be done by the start of the tax year. So if you make an election now, it will not apply until 6 April 1999. However, if you married during the 1997/98 tax year and made an election by 5 April 1998, this will apply for the 1997/98 tax year.

This election will remain until it is revoked.

You must make an election by notifying your (or her) Tax Office in writing. Ask for form 18.

Special rules for those aged 65 or over

Although you can alter the way the married couple's allowance is given, you can only split the basic married couple's allowance of £1830. The remainder of the higher age-rated married couple's allowance must always be given to the husband. So if you qualify for a married couple's allowance of £3185, only the first £1830 can be given to the wife; the remaining £1355 must still be given to the husband.

However, if you cannot use up your allowance (because you do not have sufficient income) you can transfer any surplus allowance to your wife. For instance, if you have an income of £6000 and are over 65, you will have allowances of £8403 (£5220 basic plus the £3185 married couples' allowance). You will have £2405 of unused allowances. The first £1830 of married couples allowance can go to your spouse. The remaining surplus of £575 can be transferred by filling in boxes **16.25** and **16.26**.

Tax warning: Although you can claim the higher age-related allowances if you or your wife was aged 65 or over during the tax year (on or before 5 April 1998) these allowances will be reduced if your income was over £15,600 for the tax year.

Your allowances will be reduced by £1 for every £2 of income over £15,600. So if you have income of more than £19,600 you will exceed this *earnings restriction* by £4000. So your allowances will be reduced by £2000 (£1 for every £2 of income). Your personal allowance will be reduced first. However, your age-related personal allowance cannot be reduced to less than the basic personal allowance of £4045.

So if you are 65 and have an age-related personal allowance of £5220, and have income of £19,600 (as in the example above), your allowance should be reduced to £3220 (£5025 – £2000). As this is below £4045 you will be given a basic personal allowance of £4045 and the remainder of the reduction (£4045 – £3220= £825) will be used to reduce your married couple's allowance. As you are over 65 this is £3185. So £3185 – £825 = £2360. Once again, your age-related married couple's allowance cannot be reduced to less than the basic married couple's allowance of £1830. For further explanation see the Allowances section in Chapter 2.

Tax tip: If you are claiming the age allowance and earn more than £15,600 you may benefit from switching some of your income to your wife (but you have to give it to her as an outright gift and it must be in her name). This is because you lose £1 of age-related allowance for every £2 of income over £15,600. You will lose **all** of the extra age-related personal and married couple's allowances if you have an income of more than £20,660 (if you are both aged over 65 but under 75). If you switch some of your income to your wife, you will have less income to take into account when working out the reduction in your age-related allowances. If you reduce your income to £15,600, you will not suffer any earnings reduction in your age allowances.

Married and separated women: married couple's allowance

■ ***Married couple's allowance for a married woman** - see page 24 of your Tax Return Guide.*

- Date of marriage (if after 5 April 1997) **16.11** [/ /]
- Husband's full name **16.12** [ ]
- Tick box 16.13 if you or your husband have allocated **half** the allowance to you **16.13** [ ]
- Husband's tax reference (if known, please) **16.14** [ ]
- Tick box 16.15 if you and your husband have allocated **all** the allowance to you **16.15** [ ]

Even if you are married, or were married, during the tax year you may not have to fill in this section. You should only fill it in if:

- ❑ you have agreed with your Tax Office that you can claim **half** of the married couple's allowance;
- ❑ you have agreed with your **husband** and your Tax Office that you can claim **all** of the married couple's allowance.

You can only make a claim if you were married and living with your husband (or living apart but with no intention to separate) for all or part of the tax year ended 5 April 1998.

Box 16.11:

Only fill this in if you married after 5 April 1997.

Boxes 16.12 and 16.14:

Write your husband's full name and his tax reference if you know this.

Tax tips:

- ❑ Do **not** fill in box **16.11** if you are still entitled to claim half or all of the married couple's allowance from a previous marriage. This is because you will only be able to claim all or half the married couple's allowance for your new marriage from the date you married. If you continue to make the claim for your old marriage you can claim your share of the married couple's allowance for the whole tax year. This will only usually apply if you were married then quickly divorced and remarried.
- ❑ Do **not** fill in box **16.11** if you were entitled to claim the additional personal allowance (which is the same as the married couple's allowance) because you were unmarried and had a child living with you before the tax year during the tax year. This is because you can claim the additional personal allowance for the entire tax year, but can only claim all (or your share) of the married couple's allowance from the date you married.

Boxes 16.13 and 16.15:

The married couple's allowance automatically goes to the husband. Although the wife can claim half the allowance **without** his consent, she **must** agree this with her Tax Office **before** the start of the tax year. However, if you married during the tax year you can make the election to split the married couple's allowance for the first year of marriage provided you do this by the end of the tax year.

> **Tax tip:** If your husband has insufficient income to use up his allowances (his income is less than his allowances) you can claim his surplus allowances. Fill in boxes **16.25** to **16.28**.

Special rules for those newly widowed

If your husband died during the tax year ended 5 April 1998, you can claim any part of the married couple's allowance which could not be offset against his income. So for this to apply, his income must have been less than the married couple's allowance. This applies even if you had previously agreed for you to claim all or half of the married couple's allowance.

Married men and women

> **Tax tip:** Now that the married couple's allowance is restricted to 15 per cent tax relief, there is no point in switching it from husband to wife if the wife is a higher-rate taxpayer and the husband a basic-rate taxpayer. However, if the husband is a *non-earner* he should switch all of his allowance to his wife so she can benefit from the 15 per cent tax relief on £1830 of earnings = £275. The same applies to the blind person's allowance.

■ ***Additional personal allowance*** *(available in some circumstances if you have a child living with you - see page 24 of your Tax Return Guide).*

- Name of the child claimed for **16.16** [ ]
- Child's date of birth **16.17** [/ /]
- Tick if child lives with you **16.18** [ ]
- Name of university etc/type of training if the child is 16 or over on 6 April 1997 and in full time education or training **16.19** [ ]

Those with a dependent child living with them: Additional Personal Allowance

Allowance: £1830 restricted to 15 per cent tax relief (giving a tax saving of £275).

Many people do not know that they can claim this allowance and so it can be overlooked. However, even if you have forgotten to claim in the past, remember you can backdate your claim for six years.

You can claim the allowance if you are unmarried, separated, divorced or widowed throughout the tax year **and** have a dependent child living with you.

You can claim this allowance even if the child only lives with you for part of the year. If the child lives with both you and your former spouse or partner you can split the allowance.

Rules for women

You can still claim the allowance even if you remarried or were reconciled with your husband during the tax year ended 5 April 1998 provided the child lived with you for the part of the year in which you were single, separated, divorced or widowed. (See p. 85 for the married couple's allowance Tax Tips.)

Rules for men

You can also claim the allowance if you separated permanently from your wife in the year ended 5 April 1998 but a child lived with you after you separated **and** you are not getting all the married couple's allowance. You can also claim the allowance if you married during the tax year (either remarried or married the mother of the child) and decided to claim this additional personal allowance instead of the married couple's allowance. (See p. 85 for the married couple's allowance Tax Tips.)

Note: You cannot claim the full married couple's allowance and the full additional personal allowance if you separate during the year. The maximum you can get is the **lower of**:

- ❑ the share of the additional personal allowance you are entitled to when the full amount is shared with someone else; **or**

- the full amount of additional personal allowance **after** deducting any share of the married couple's allowance you may be entitled to.

Married men get an extra concession if their wife was unable to look after herself at all because of illness or disablement for the **whole** of the tax year. They can claim the full additional personal allowance and the full married couple's allowance.

Married men who separated from their wives before 6 April 1991 and who are still entitled to married couple's allowance from that marriage cannot get any additional personal allowance.

To qualify for the allowance the child must:

- be your own child, a stepchild, legitimated child or a child you legally adopted before he or she was 18;
- be a child under 16 on 6 April 1997 who you look after at your own expense;
- be over 16 but under 18 on 6 April 1997 **and** either in full-time education at school, college or university or receiving full-time training for at least two years for a trade or profession.

Note: You can only get one allowance even if more than one child lives with you.

Boxes 16.16 and 16.17:

Write in the name of the child claimed for and the child's date of birth. If you are claiming for more than one child, you must always write the name and age of the **youngest** child unless someone else is claiming for that child.

Box 16.18:

Tick this box if the child lives with you (even if for only part of the year).

Box 16.19:

If the child was 16 or over on 6 April 1997 (but under 18) write in the name of the university, school or college or the full-time training scheme the child attends.

Boxes 16.20 to 16.23:

Sharing a claim
Name and address of other person claiming

16.20

Postcode

- Enter your share as a percentage 16.21 %
- If share not agreed, enter the number of days in the year ended 5 April 1998 that the child lived with
  - you 16.22 days
  - other person 16.23 days

These boxes are for those sharing a claim. For example, a divorced couple may share custody of their children and can therefore share the allowance.

If you have agreed a set share of the allowance, write this in box **16.21**. You must use a percentage. So if you can claim two-thirds of the allowance write 67.

Write the name and address of the other person in box **16.20.**

If you have not agreed a split, in box **16.22** write the number of days the child lived with you and in box **16.23** the number of days the child lived with the other person.

Tax tips:

- ❑ If you are not married, but live together as husband and wife, you can only claim one allowance (for the youngest child) between you, however many children you have. However, you can split the allowance so you get half each.
- ❑ If you are **not** living together as husband and wife and both look after more than one child, one of you may be able to claim for a different child instead of both claiming for the youngest. So you **both** get the full amount of allowance and do **not** have to split the allowance.

Box 16.24: Widow's bereavement allowance

■ ***Widow's bereavement allowance***

- Date of your husband's death 16.24 / /

Allowance: £1830 restricted to 15 per cent tax relief (giving a tax saving of £275).

This allowance is given in the year of your husband's death and, provided you do not remarry before the beginning of the following tax year, for the year following your husband's death. So if you were widowed during the tax year or your husband died in the previous tax year ending 5 April 1997 (and you did not remarry in that year) claim this allowance by writing the date of your husband's death in box **16.24**.

Note: This allowance is only given to widows, **not** widowers.

> **Tax tip:** If in the year of your husband's death he had insufficient income to use up the married couple's allowance the 'unused' surplus will **automatically** be passed to you as the widow. You do not have to make an election. However, if all or part of the married couple's allowance was transferred to you, the widow, by election before your husband's death, that married couple's allowance will be transferred back to the husband.

Boxes 16.25 to 16.28: Transfer of surplus allowances

■ ***Transfer of surplus allowances*** *- see page 25 of your Tax Return Guide before you fill in boxes 16.25 to 16.28.*

- Tick if you want your spouse to have your unused allowances **16.25**
- Tick if you want to have your spouse's unused allowances **16.26**

Please give details in the 'Additional information' box on page 8 *- see page 25 of your Tax Return Guide for what is needed.*

If you want to calculate your tax, enter the amount of the surplus allowance you can have.

- Blind person's **surplus** allowance **16.27** £
- Married couple's **surplus** allowance **16.28** £

This section may appear to be a little technical, but it is worth understanding how you can save tax by transferring *surplus* or *unused allowances*.

Only those who are married and do not earn as much, in the tax year as the total of all their allowances can benefit. So if your income was £4000 and your allowances were £5875 (£4045 for the basic allowance and £1830 for the married couple's allowance) you will have *unused* allowances that have not been used to reduce your taxable income. Remember allowances can only reduce your taxable income to zero – any unused amount of allowance is not then used to give you a tax rebate.

The only *unused* allowances that can be transferred are the married couple's allowance and the blind person's allowance. Although, if you are a husband whose income does not use up all of the personal allowance **and** your wife received the transitional allowance in 1995/96, you may, in certain circumstances, be able to transfer unused personal allowances to her.

You must have lived with your spouse for at least part of the tax year in order to transfer any unused allowance.

If you want to transfer any surplus married couple's or blind person's allowance or the transitional allowance, tick box **16.25.** If you are unsure if you will have any unused allowances, add up your income and then add up your allowances. If your income is roughly equal or less than the amount of allowances you think you are entitled to, tick the box. Your Tax Office will then work out the surplus.

Likewise, if you think your spouse's income will be less than their allowances, you can ask for these unused allowances to be transferred and used to reduce your tax bill. You can do this by ticking box **16.26.**

Notes:

- ❑ If you tick box **16.25** or **16.26** you **must** then write your spouse's name, address, tax reference, National Insurance number and Tax Office in the 'Additional information' box on page 8 of your Tax Return.

A step-by-step guide to filling in the remainder of the eight pages of your main Tax Return including Q17 to Q23, is given in Part 5 of this book, while a Tax Calculation Guide is provided in Appendix 1. The reason why you cannot fill in the remainder of your main Tax Return at this stage is that you will not know what information to include until you have filled in the supplementary pages.

PART
3

EMPLOYMENT

These two pages of the Tax Return should be filled in by those who were in employment during the tax year from 6 April 1996 to 5 April 1998. You must fill them in if you answered ***YES*** to Q1 on page 2 of your main Tax Return.

A different form has to be filled in for each employment. So if you have had three different jobs during the year, you will need to fill in three different forms.

PAPERWORK

- ❑ Your P60 Certificate of Pay, Income Tax and National Insurance contributions which your employer should give you/or have given you by 31 May 1998. If you had more than one job, your pay from that previous job will **not** be included on your P60.
- ❑ If you left a job during the tax year, your P45 (Part 1A).
- ❑ Also your P11D, P9D or other information from your employer about benefits and expenses (such as company cars). This should be given to you/or have been given to you by your employer by 6 July 1998.
- ❑ Your notice of Tax Coding if you have been sent one by the Inland Revenue. This will tell you which employee benefits you are paying tax on.
- ❑ And details of any business expenses.
- ❑ Your pay slips if you are missing any of the above forms.

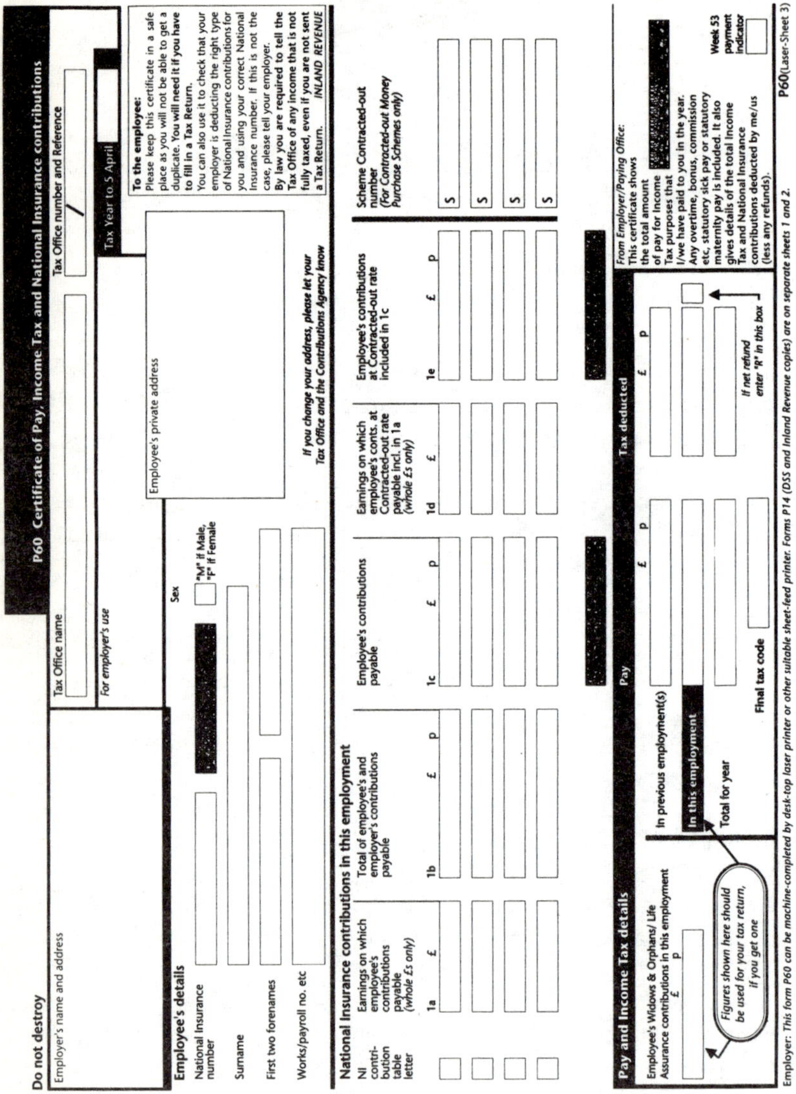

Do not destroy

P60 Certificate of Pay, Income Tax and National Insurance contributions

Employer's name and address

Tax Office name

Tax Office number and Reference /

For employer's use

Tax Year to 5 April

To the employee:
Please keep this certificate in a safe place as you will not be able to get a duplicate. **You will need it if you have to fill in a Tax Return.**
You can also use it to check that your employer is deducting the right type of National Insurance contributions for you and using your correct National Insurance number. If this is not the case, please tell your employer.
By law you are required to tell the Tax Office of any income that is not fully taxed, even if you are not sent a Tax Return. *INLAND REVENUE*

Employee's details

National Insurance number

Sex: "M" if Male, "F" if Female

Surname

First two forenames

Works/payroll no. etc

Employee's private address

If you change your address, please let your Tax Office and the Contributions Agency know

National Insurance contributions in this employment

NI contri-bution table letter	1a Earnings on which employee's contributions payable (*whole £s only*) £	1b Total of employee's and employer's contributions payable £ p	1c Employee's contributions payable £ p	1d Earnings on which employee's conts. at Contracted-out rate payable incl. in 1a (*whole £s only*) £	1e Employee's contributions at Contracted-out rate included in 1c £ p	Scheme Contracted-out number (*For Contracted-out Money Purchase Schemes only*)
						S
						S
						S
						S

Pay and Income Tax details

Employee's Widows & Orphans/ Life Assurance contributions in this employment £ p

Figures shown here should be used for your tax return, if you get one

	Pay £ p	Tax deducted £ p
In previous employment(s)		
In this employment		
Total for year		

If net refund enter "R" in this box

Final tax code

From Employer/Paying Office:
This certificate shows the total amount of pay for Income Tax purposes that I/we have paid to you in the year. Any overtime, bonus, commission etc, statutory sick pay or statutory maternity pay is included. It also gives details of the total Income Tax and National Insurance contributions deducted by me/us (less any refunds).

Week 53 payment indicator

Employer: *This form P60 can be machine-completed by desk-top laser printer or other suitable sheet-feed printer. Forms P14 (DSS and Inland Revenue copies) are on separate sheets 1 and 2.* P60(Laser-Sheet 3)

Most figures only have to be copied from the documents listed. If you have more than one figure to fit into each box, you will have to add the figures up. So have a calculator to hand. **Once again, remember to ignore pence when writing figures.**

10

EMPLOYER'S DETAILS AND PAY

EMPLOYMENT DETAILS

Employer's PAYE reference
1.1

Employer's name
1.2

Date employment started
1.3 / /

Date finished
1.4 / /

Employer's address
1.5

Postcode

Tick box 1.6 if you were a director of the company
1.6

and, if so, tick box 1.7 if it was a close company
1.7

Boxes 1.1 and 1.2: Employer's PAYE reference and name

Copy the PAYE reference number on your P60 or Part 1A of your P45. If you work for a subsidiary of a large company and, as such, are confused about which name to use, copy the name on your P60.

Box 1.3: Date employment started:

This should only be filled in if you started a new job in the tax year between 6 April 1997 and 5 April 1998. If not, leave it blank.

Box 1.4: Date finished:

This should only be filled in if you stopped working during the tax year. Copy the date listed on Part 1A of your P45.

Box 1.5: Employer's address:

Again copy the one listed on your P60.

Box 1.6: Company directors:

Tick this if you were employed as a director of a company during the tax year.

Box 1.7: Directors of a close company:

You should know if your company is a close (or closed) company but if you don't, it generally means a company that is under the control of its directors (where the directors are also shareholders) or companies with five or fewer shareholders. If you are still in doubt ask your Tax Office for guidance.

INCOME FROM EMPLOYMENT

Remember only to include pay received in the 6 April 1997 to 5 April 1998 tax year. Income from employment is taxable when you receive it. If you are entitled to pay – but do not actually receive it or take it until a later date – you will be taxed on that pay on the date you were entitled to it. So if you are entitled to a payment on 1 April but do not receive it until 21 April, you must include it in the tax year ending 5 April. However, if you receive payment early – before work is completed – you will be taxed on the date you received it.

Box 1.8: Payments:

- Payments from P60 (or P45 or pay slips) — Before tax: 1.8 £

This is listed as total pay on your P60 (or P45). If there is more than one figure, the one you need is 'net pay after superannuation' (you do not pay tax on earnings invested in your company pension scheme) or 'total pay this employment' or 'pay for tax purposes'. If you had more than one job or were unemployed there may be figures in the 'previous employment' box. These should **not** be included on this form – remember you need to have a separate form for each type of employment.

> **Warning:** Take care if you were unemployed during the year. Income support or Jobseeker's Allowance may be included in the 'pay from previous employment' box on your P60. Do not include these as part of your salary. Any unemployment or other benefit should be written in box **11.5** on your Tax Return.

Your payments figure in box **1.8** should include:

- ❑ wages (excluding any tax-free profit-related pay)
- ❑ holiday pay
- ❑ statutory sick pay and maternity pay (if paid by your employer)
- ❑ commissions
- ❑ overtime
- ❑ fees
- ❑ bonuses and other voluntary payments

after deducting:

- ❑ money donated to a payroll giving scheme
- ❑ contributions to your employer's pension scheme
- ❑ any profit-related pay.

Do **not** include any lump-sum redundancy payments.

> **Tax tips:**
>
> - ❑ You can receive some pay free of tax. If you were in a registered profit-related scheme during the 1997/98 tax year you could receive pay tax free up to a ceiling of £4000 or 20 per cent of your total pay, whichever is the lower. However, this is now being phased out. The 20 per cent limit remains but the maximum amount you can receive has been reduced to £2000 from 1 January 1998 and will fall to £1000 on 1 January 1999. It will be phased out on 1 January 2000. So make the most of it while you can.

- ❑ Another way to receive pay free of tax is by asking your employer to set up a staff suggestion scheme. You can receive 50 per cent of the first year's expected net benefit of the scheme or 10 per cent of the benefit over five years with an overall maximum tax-free sum of £5000. To qualify, the scheme must be a formal scheme open to all employees and the suggestion must be outside your normal job – and adopted by the employer. So if you work in the marketing department you cannot get a tax-free sum for suggesting a saving in the marketing budget, but you can if you suggest a way for the company to save money on its general postage or telephone bills.
- ❑ You automatically receive tax relief at your highest rate of tax on all contributions made to your employer's pension scheme. Make the most of this tax benefit. Tax relief on pensions may be reduced in future so consider topping up your contributions by making extra contributions through the scheme's additional voluntary contribution (AVC) provisions.

Special notes for employees

You must include all the income received in the tax year as an employee even if you earned it in an earlier tax year or you have been paid in advance for work not yet done. You should also include pay that you were entitled to receive but have not yet been paid.

Special notes for directors

All income received in the tax year must be included in the payments boxes even if you earned the money in an earlier tax year or have been paid for work not yet done. You should also include sums that were due to you but which you arranged to receive in some other way. Payment is treated as being received on the **earliest** of the following:

- ❑ the date you were paid or payment on account was made;
- ❑ the date you became entitled to be paid or paid on account even if you were paid later;
- ❑ the date money was credited to you in the company's accounts or records even if you were not able to draw on the money at the time; and
- ❑ the date earnings for a particular period were decided (unless they were decided before the period of work ended).

• Payments not on P60 etc	- tips	1.9	£
	- other payments (excluding expenses shown below and lump sums and compensation payments or benefits shown overleaf)	1.10	£

Boxes 1.9 and 1.10: Other payments:

These include tips and any other payments not included on the P60 (or P45 Part 1A or payslips). Do **not** include redundancy or other lump-sum payments, expenses, loans or money for petrol. Include all income that is from or related to your work but not included in box **1.8**. In box **1.9** you should include tips and gratuities.

Warning: The Inland Revenue has a good idea of the amount of tips given to each type of worker – waiter, hairdresser, taxi driver, etc. So, if you try to cheat, this may be easily spotted.

Tax tip: If you receive a one-off gift that is genuinely a present (not instead of pay for work) and this costs your employer £100 or less, this will be tax free. Gifts to mark a personal event such as a marriage are also tax free.

The following ***must*** be included in the 'Other payments' box:

- ❑ golden hellos – inducements to take up new employment;
- ❑ payments given to compensate or reward you for changes in your conditions of service or employment – so if you agree to work longer hours or give up your company car and get a one-off payment to compensate you for this it must be included here;
- ❑ loans written off or cancelled because you completed some employment condition – for example, you have worked for an agreed period of service;
- ❑ payments which are not for work done but by virtue of your employment – for example your company gives you some money to go on holiday;
- ❑ incentive awards – write in the gross amount (before tax is deducted). The tax paid should be included in **1.11**;
- ❑ sums from an approved profit-sharing scheme but **not** profit-related pay;

- ❑ payments for agreeing to restrict your activities – for example agreeing not to compete with the business of your former employer – also known as golden handcuffs.

1.10: Tax deducted:

Write in the amount deducted from your payments in boxes **1.8** to **1.10.**

You should find this figure on your P60 (or P45). If you had tax refunded to you, put the amount in brackets.

11

EMPLOYEE BENEFITS AND EXPENSES

Benefits (also known as benefits-in-kind) generally mean the perks that go with your job – such as a company car, free private health insurance or a subsidized mortgage.

> **Warning:** Although you can copy most figures from your P11D, you must check this carefully as you are responsible for what you enter on your Tax Return.

Some items may have been left off your P11D – this may be because they are **exempt** from tax (see list on page 104). In other cases your employer may have a dispensation from the Inland Revenue (see expenses dispensations on page 119).

HOW EMPLOYEE BENEFITS ARE TAXED

To help you fill in the boxes below, here is a quick guide to the taxation of employee perks – known as *benefits in kind*. Generally all benefits – any perk you get because of your employment – are taxable unless they are exempt (tax free). Tax is always charged at the *highest rate* of Income Tax you pay. So if your perk has a cash equivalent (often the cost to the employer) of £1000, as a higher-rate taxpayer you will be charged 40 per cent tax and pay £400 in tax.

Special rules for employees earning under £8500

You pay less tax on benefits if you earn under £8500 a year. This earnings figure must **include** the value of benefits and expenses. These rules do **not** apply to company directors and those who control more than 5 per cent of the share capital of the company. Boxes **1.16** to **1.23** do **not** have to be filled in if you earn under £8500.

How to calculate if you earn £8500 or more

Take your basic salary, add any bonuses, commissions and other financial payments. Then add the taxable value of any benefit – this is also known as the cash equivalent. So if you earn £7000 a year and get a company car with a taxable value of £1400, private medical insurance worth £150 and a mobile phone worth £200, you are treated as though you earn £8750 a year. And therefore the tax concessions given to those earning under £8500 do **not** apply to you even though your basic salary is only £7000 a year.

Note that the earnings are worked out on an annual basis. If you were only employed for part of the year, you must work out the figures as though you worked for the whole year.

Which employee benefits are tax free?

Generally to escape tax on employee benefits and expenses they must be *wholly, exclusively and necessarily incurred in the performance* of duties of office or employment. The 'in performance of duties' is very important. You cannot claim travelling from home to work because your duties of employment do not start until the place of work is reached. However, the following benefits are exempt from tax.

- ❑ **Canteens**: tea and coffee and also free or cheap meals provided these are available to all employees (even if the management has its own coffee area or restaurant).
- ❑ **Meal/luncheon vouchers** – provided they are not worth more than 15p a day.
- ❑ Child care in a **workplace nursery** but not (in the tax year 1997/98) nursery place vouchers or free or subsidized places at nurseries away from the workplace.
- ❑ **Medical check-ups** provided these are routine or paid for by your employer.

- ❑ **Pension scheme contributions** made by your employer into approved company pension schemes.
- ❑ Any **perks that do not cost your employer** money or do not incur an additional cost. For instance, you work for an airline, theatre, bus or train company and your employer gives you a subsidized seat.
- ❑ **Sports facilities** provided they are available to employees generally and not small groups of staff.
- ❑ **Incidental expenses** while you are working away from home – for things like telephone calls home and laundry. You can receive £5 for every night spent away from home on business in the UK and £10 if you are abroad. However, if you get more than this you cannot claim this amount tax free – the **total** amount then becomes taxable.
- ❑ Directors' and employees' **liability insurance** if it is paid by your employer.
- ❑ **Training expenses** if you need to acquire new skills for your job. The expenses can include books, travel to and from the course and the reasonable cost of meals.
- ❑ **Clothes** specially needed for work (but not everyday work clothes such as suits) and the cost of cleaning or repairing protective or functional clothing.
- ❑ **Discounts on goods and services** – say, for instance, you work for a shop and get cheap goods at the wholesale price – provided it does not cost your employer any money.
- ❑ **Employee parties and outings** including staff Christmas parties – normally the maximum allowed is £75 per head.
- ❑ Provision of travel, accommodation and subsistence due to disruption caused by industrial action.
- ❑ The value of **outplacement counselling** services provided in the UK to full-time employees (with a minimum two years' service) who are made redundant.
- ❑ Fees and **subscriptions to professional bodies** – provided the organization is Inland Revenue approved and you need to be a member for your job.
- ❑ **Personal gifts** on marriage or retirement (but not money on retirement).
- ❑ **Relocation expenses** are tax free within limits – generally up to £8000 if you have to move home (it is no longer within reasonable daily travelling distance from your employment). Costs that can be paid for include: removal, legal, estate agency and even the costs of buying new domestic goods if the old ones are not suitable for your new home.

- ❑ **Season ticket loans** and other **interest-free or cheap loans** up to a total of £5000.
- ❑ **Life insurance** provided it is part of your company pension scheme
- ❑ Some low-rent or rent-free **job-related living accommodation** – if it is necessary for your job (for instance if you are a caretaker) or it enables you to do your job better (for instance, a publican) or you have to live in it for security reasons.
- ❑ **Long-service awards** if given for service of 20 years or more with the same employer (no more than £20 per year of service – so that is £400 for the minimum 20 years).
- ❑ Scholarship and **apprenticeship** schemes provided you are enrolled for a least one academic year and attend full time for an average of at least 20 weeks a year and the amount of payment including your lodging, travelling and subsistence but excluding tuition fees is not above £7000. If you receive more, the full amount is taxable.
- ❑ **Shares** bought cheaply or given for free in your employer's company through an approved share company share scheme – these include profit sharing, share option and SAYE share option (Save As You Earn) schemes.
- ❑ **Staff suggestion schemes** up to an overall maximum of £5000 for the scheme.
- ❑ **Late-night travel costs** from work provided it is after 9pm and public transport is difficult (but this cannot be paid on a regular basis).
- ❑ Cost of maintaining and repairing **tools and instruments** including musical instruments needed for work.
- ❑ **Mileage payments** for using your own car for business under the fixed profit car scheme.
- ❑ **Books** needed for work.
- ❑ Some of the **heating and lighting costs of your home** and some of the **telephone bills** and other costs if you **have** to use your home for work. You may also be able to claim some of the rent.

> **Tax tip:** Make sure you are familiar with the benefits you can receive tax free and use this information to make sure you claim every tax-free benefit you can and when negotiating any additional benefits with your employer.

HOW THE TAX ON BENEFITS IS CALCULATED

Benefits and perks are taxed on their value or cost to the employer – this is known as the *cash equivalent.* If you pay towards the cost of the benefit, the amount you pay is often deducted from the taxable value or cash equivalent although in some cases you must reimburse the total costs to escape tax. In some cases you are taxed on a fixed amount regardless of how much the perk costs your employer. For instance, the cash equivalent or taxable value of mobile phones is a fixed £200.

Warning:

- ❑ You can no longer write 'as per employer's return' on your Tax Return and expect the Inland Revenue to track down the figures. You must write in all the figures yourself, unless your employer has a dispensation.
- ❑ The Inland Revenue may ask you to provide receipts or records (particularly for business mileage) to ensure that you are not cheating on your tax.

Box 1.12: Assets transferred/payments made for you:

	Amount
• Assets transferred/ payments made for you	1.12 £

The assets referred to are anything your employer gives you that can either be converted into cash or sold – also known as payments in kind. Note that this does not include assets that you are only given the use of but which remain the property of your employer (these go in box **1.22**.) You are taxed on the second-hand value of the asset or the cost of the item to your employer (including any installation costs), whichever is the greater – less any amount you paid for it. Employees earning less than £8500 a year (including benefits and expenses) will only be charged tax on the second-hand value. The figures should be included on your P11D.

The type of 'assets' that are covered by this box include:

- television sets;
- furniture;
- clothing.

If you are given something you have already had the use of, the rules are different. You are taxed on the market value when you are given the asset **or** the market value of the asset when it was first loaned to you less the amount of tax that has already been charged.

However, this rule does **not** apply to cars, telephones or mobile phones. In this case you will be taxed on the second-hand value when you were given the asset less anything you pay for it.

> **Warning:** If your employer gives you your company car when you leave employment, you will be taxed on its second-hand value (determined by the Inland Revenue), minus anything you paid your employer.

The types of 'payments' you should enter in box **1.12** include bills paid directly by your employer on your behalf:

- your personal telephone bill paid directly to the telephone company;
- your rent paid to your landlord;
- your personal credit card bill paid directly to the credit card company.

Box 1.13: Vouchers, credit cards and tokens

	Amount
• Vouchers/credit cards	1.13 £

These include company credit or charge cards or vouchers for goods and services (other than tax-free vouchers such as luncheon or gift vouchers and, until the start of this year, car parking vouchers). Note that vouchers used to pay for running company cars or vans are taxed elsewhere. The value of these will be included in your P11D unless your employer has a dispensation. If you use vouchers or credit cards to meet work expenses, the total value should be written here and you can then claim the amount you spent on company or work expenses in boxes **1.32** to **1.35**.

Tax tip: If your employer gives you a credit or charge card to pay for business expenses and this is a taxable fringe benefit you do not have to pay tax on any annual card fee or interest paid by your employer. If the card does not count as a taxable benefit (it was used wholly, exclusively and necessarily for business) you will not pay any tax at all.

Box 1.14: Living accommodation

	Amount
• Living accommodation	1.14 £

Enter in the value of any accommodation you or your family get because of your job. Again your employer should give you the figure. (See the list of tax-free benefits on page 104 if you are unsure about whether or not your accommodation is taxable.)

If it is taxable you will be taxed on either the rateable value or the rent paid for the property, whichever is the higher, less anything you pay for the accommodation. If the property cost more than £75,000 and the tax is based on rateable value you may have to pay extra tax. Ask for Help Sheet *IR202: Living accommodation* for more information.

USING YOUR OWN CAR ON COMPANY BUSINESS

Box 1.15: Mileage allowances

	Amount
• Mileage allowance	1.15 £

If you get paid a mileage allowance for using your own car for business journeys this will be tax free provided it is within certain allowed limits. **You only have to enter a figure in this box if you receive more than is allowed** (see Table 11.1). And if you receive more than is allowed, you must **only enter the amount in excess of the tax-free allowance.**

If you are in a *fixed profit car scheme* you should get details of the profit figures (amounts in excess of the mileage rate agreed by the Inland Revenue) from your employer on form P11D. If your employer gives you a profit figure you must include it.

Table 11.1 *Tax-free mileage allowance for 1997/98 for employees using their own car on business*

Engine size	Maximum reimbursement per mile First 4000 business miles	Excess over 4000 business miles
Up to 1000cc	28p	17p
1001–1500cc	35p	20p
1501–2000cc	45p	25p
Over 2000cc	63p	36p

If your employer is not in a fixed profit scheme, you can calculate whether or not you have to pay tax by using Table 11.1.

To calculate if you need to put a profit figure in box **1.5** follow this example:

Mr M drives a 2000cc car. He drives 6000 business miles a year, and his company pays him 42p a mile.

42p per mile x 6000 business miles = total received from his employer **£2520**

Under the *mileage allowance* he is allowed:

4000 business miles x **45p** per mile allowed tax free = **£1800**

The remainder of his business miles (over the 4000 limit) can only be claimed at a lower rate (see Table 11.1):

+ **2000** business miles x **25p** per mile allowed tax free = **£500**

Total allowed = £1800 + £500 = **£2300**

So he has made a profit of £2520 – £2300 = **£220**

This £220 is the profit figure he should include in box **1.15**.

Tax tip: If the mileage allowance you receive is **less** than the amount you are allowed to receive tax free (see Table 11.1) you can claim the extra amount that you are entitled to in box **1.32.** So if you are entitled to receive a mileage allowance of £1800 tax free but only received £1000, you can claim the additional £800 tax-free allowance from the Inland Revenue instead of your employer.

The mileage allowance is known as the *quick basis* way of calculating your motoring costs because all you need to record is your business mileage.

You can opt to claim motoring costs on a more *exact basis* **instead of** the mileage allowance. In this case you will be able to claim the cost of fuel used on business journeys **and** some of the running costs including maintenance, insurance and road tax. You should keep detailed records of costs and business and private mileage.

To work out the *business proportion* – the amount you can claim back under the exact basis – total up your mileage for the year. Then calculate the miles on business:

So if you clocked up 10,000 miles in a year and 2000 of these were business miles, your business proportion will be:

$^{2000}/_{10000} = {}^{1}/_{5}$

So you can deduct one-fifth of your total costs.

Tax tips:

- ❑ Depending on your circumstances, the *exact basis* – although more time consuming – may be more tax efficient as it calculates the costs of running your car for business use more accurately. Even if your employer is in a fixed profit car scheme you can opt to calculate your mileage profit on either an exact or quick basis.
- ❑ If you do **not** claim a mileage allowance, there are other tax advantages. You may be able to claim for some of the costs of buying the car in box **1.35**.

Boxes 1.16 to 1.23

You **don't** have to fill these boxes if you earn under **£8500** (for definition and calculation see page 104) unless you were a company director.

COMPANY CARS

Boxes 1.16 and 1.17: Company cars and fuel benefits

- Company cars — 1.16 Amount £
- Fuel for company cars — 1.17 Amount £

Enter the *cash equivalent* of **cars made available to you for private use**. Private use includes driving to and from work. **Company cars are taxed at 35 per cent of the list price at the time the car was registered** and this value includes accessories. The tax applies to cars provided to you or a member of your family. So if your car has a list price of £10,000 you will taxed on the taxable value or benefit to you, known as the *cash equivalent*, which will be 35 per cent of £10,000 = £3500.

The maximum price of the car under these rules is £80,000. If you make a contribution towards the cost of buying the car, this amount (up to a maximum of £5000) can be deducted from the initial price before calculating the cash equivalent. However, if you pay your employer for **all private use** of your car you will not have to pay tax on the fuel.

If you get free fuel for **private travel** you will also have to include the benefit value of this. **Do not include cars that are for business use only such as pool cars.** To qualify as a pool car the car must be used by more than one person, not used by one person to the exclusion of others and not kept overnight near an employee's residence.

Your tax is **reduced** if you frequently use your car for business rather than as a perk. This reduction is based on your *business mileage* or the amount of miles you drive on company business during the tax year from April to April.

That is why it is essential that you keep a record of your mileage when you drive your car on company business. Table 11.2 illustrates the ways in which company car tax can be reduced.

However, if your car is over four years old, giving you a one-third reduction in your company car tax, **and** you qualify for a tax reduction because of the business mileage you drive, you must do the following calculation, for example:

Take one-third off the taxable value because the car is over four years old:

£10,000 (the list price) divided by 35% = **£3500 (taxable value)**

This is the amount you pay tax on.

£3500 (taxable value) reduced by $^1/_3$ as car is over four years old = **£2333.33**

Then make the second reduction because you do more than 18,000 business miles:

£2333.33 (the remaining taxable value) reduced by $^2/_3$ for mileage = **£778**

So you will taxed on a taxable value of £777.77 and this is the figure you should include on your Tax Return.

It does not matter in which order you do the calculation – if you reduce by two-thirds and then one-third the answer will be the same.

Note that if you have a second or subsequent car no reduction for mileage is given unless the business mileage of that second car is more than 18,000 a year, in which case the reduction is one third.

Table 11.2 *How company car tax can be reduced*

Reason for company car tax reduction	Amount of reduction
If you drive between 2500 and 17,999 business miles in the tax year	the taxable value of your car is reduced by $^1/_3$
If you drive 18,000 or more business miles in the tax year	the taxable value of your car is reduced by $^2/_3$ (this replaces the $^1/_3$ figure above)
If your car was over four years old at the end the tax year (5 April 1997)	the taxable value of your car is reduced by $^1/_3$
If you pay towards the cost of buying your company car	the taxable value is reduced by the amount you pay your employer
If you have use of the car for only part of the year	the taxable value is reduced by the proportion of the year you had use of the car (so if it was six months it will be reduced by half)
If you are disabled and the car has been modified to meet your special needs	the costs of installing modifications are deducted from the taxable value

Tax tips:

- ❑ If possible try to drive at least 2500 business miles a year to save on tax. That way you will qualify for a one-third reduction in your company car tax. And if you are approaching 18,000 business miles a year, try to drive at least this amount of mileage to qualify for a two-thirds reduction in your tax.
- ❑ Your company car cash equivalent is reduced if you make a contribution to its purchase. However, any contributions beyond £5000 are ignored – so do not pay any more than this.
- ❑ If your car is to be renewed, consider one with a cheaper taxable value – that way you will pay less tax.
- ❑ If your company car is over four years old, think twice before renewing it as cars over four years old qualify for a one-third reduction in company car tax. Note that to qualify as being four years old the car must be four years old at the **end** of the tax year. The car's 'age' starts on the date it is first registered.

Tax warnings:

- ❑ It is a myth that you can use a classic car to get round these rules. Paying tax on 35 per cent of an old car's original list price would give great savings, but the Inland Revenue gets round this. If a car is 15 years old (from the time of first registration) at the end of the tax year and has a market value of £15,000 or more, you will be taxed on its market value on the last day of the tax year (subject to a ceiling of £80,000), not its original list price.
- ❑ You cannot get round the list price rules by buying a basic model and adding expensive accessories. The price you are taxed on will include any accessories fitted before the car was made available to you and any accessories worth more than £100 fitted after you received the car.

CAR OR CASH?

The system of taxing company cars means you are taxed on more than the whole price of the car over three years (35 per cent of the list price x three years = 105 per cent). But the amount of tax you actually pay is far lower. A higher rate tax payer only pays 42 per cent of the actual cost over three years.

The benefit of a company car is that you only pay tax on this cash equivalent. So if the car has a list price of £10,000, you pay tax on 35 per cent of this or £3500. Even as a higher-rate taxpayer you will only pay 40 per cent of £3500 = **£1400 tax a year**. Buying a £10,000 car could cost you far more than that (although if you use a private car for business you can deduct some of the purchasing costs).

If you were lucky enough to receive a £10,000 pay rise instead of a company car you would pay 40 per cent tax on £10,000 = **£4000 tax a year**. Even a more modest pay rise of £5000 would result in a £2000 tax bill – more than the tax on the company car.

In addition to the tax savings/losses on opting for cash or a car, you must weigh up the benefits of having a company car. Not only does your employer arrange and pay for maintenance, road tax, insurance, servicing and often membership of a motoring organization, you pay **no** tax on this extra benefit. This is a valuable perk, as the costs of running a car quickly mount up.

And also look at whether the extra salary will cover the costs of buying your own car. If you hardly ever use your company car and do not plan to buy your own car, the extra pay may be worthwhile. But if you are planning to buy your own car you could be out of pocket.

Tax warning: Note that if you take pay instead of a car, you may have to pay National Insurance contributions on this extra pay (you do not pay National Insurance contributions on benefits in kind such as company cars). But as you do not have to pay National Insurance contributions on earnings over £24,180 (in the 1997/98 tax year) this may not apply.

CHANGING OR LOSING YOUR COMPANY CAR

The taxable value of your car will be reduced in line with the number of days for which the car was unavailable if you stopped getting a car. If your car (the same car) was unavailable for at least 30 days a similar reduction is given.

Tax warning: If you change company cars part way through the tax year you could be caught out on the reduction in your tax because of increased business mileage – particularly if much of your business mileage is in one part of the tax year. This is because you must apportion the business mileage to the number of days each car was available. So if your first car was available for 100 days you must clock up 2500 miles (the amount that qualifies for a one-third reduction in tax) divided by 100/365 = 685 business miles in the first car, and then 2500 divided by 365 – 100/365 = 1815 business miles in the second car.

FREE FUEL FROM YOUR COMPANY

If your company gives you expenses for petrol or diesel for private use of your car, you must declare this under fuel benefits. You do not pay tax if fuel is **only** provided for business journeys. The tax depends on the engine size of your car. Table 11.3 is for the April 1997 to April 1998 tax year. Remember, you pay tax on the cash equivalent – the cash equivalent is **not** the amount of tax you pay.

Tax warning: If you make a contribution for fuel for private use, your contributions will **not** reduce the cash equivalent or amount of tax you pay **unless** you reimburse the **whole** cost of the petrol/diesel for private use.

Tax warning: If you rarely use your car for private journeys, consider paying your employer for the full cost of this private mileage to escape tax on the fuel benefit. But remember you will only gain if you pay more in tax than you receive in free petrol. So, if you are taxed at 40 per cent on £1010 of fuel benefit this will equal £404 of tax. If your employer gives you less than this amount in free petrol, you are better off reimbursing the whole amount and not paying tax.

Table 11.3 *Fuel benefits: cash equivalents for 1997/98*

Engine size	Cash equivalent for: petrol	diesel
1400cc or less	£800	£640
1401 to 2000cc	£1010	£640
Over 2000cc (or with no cylinder capacity)	£1490	£820

Box 1.18: Vans

- Vans — Amount **1.18** £

This covers those who have a van made available to them for private use. Again your employer should have given you details – the cash equivalents are at a fixed rate. If you had one van during the year and it is fairly new (registered on or after 6 April 1994) the cash equivalent is £500. Otherwise it is £350. If you have to make a payment for using the van for private use, deduct this sum from the figure. If the van was not exclusively yours for the whole of the year, the cash value is reduced proportionately – so if the van was exclusively yours for only six months you only pay half. For this to apply the van must not be exclusively yours for more than 30 days at a stretch.

Box 1.19: Interest-free and low-interest loans

- Interest-free and low-interest loans — Amount **1.19** £

You do not have to include season ticket loans or other loans if the total balance of these is £5000 or less. If the loan is above this you will pay tax on the **total** loan. The amount on which you are taxed will be the difference between what the loan would have cost you if you had to take the loan out from lender and the actual amount you pay in interest. The official rate of interest is used in these calculations to determine the amount of interest you would have paid.

Subsidized mortgages may qualify for tax relief. See Q15 of your main Tax Return.

Box 1.20: Mobile phones

	Amount
• Mobile telephones	**1.20** £

As with cars, you only have to fill in this box if the phone is available to you for **private use**. If you pay your employer for the full cost of private calls on your mobile phone you **don't** have to pay tax. Otherwise, the cash equivalent is £200 for every phone.

Box 1.21: Private medical or dental insurance

	Amount
• Private medical or dental insurance	**1.21** £

The figure generally is what this insurance costs your employer less any contributions you make.

Box 1.22: Other benefits

	Amount
• Other benefits	**1.22** £

This covers the total cash equivalent of any other benefits that are not covered in the other boxes. These could include things like:

- a chauffeur;
- any relocation expenses above £8000 that are not tax free;
- nursery place vouchers;
- Income Tax paid but not deducted (directors only); and
- other assets or service for your private use.

Copy the figures from your P11D.

Some share benefits – for example, if your employer enables you to sell shares for more than their market value – should be listed in box **1.22.** If so, they should be listed on your P11D. Otherwise most share benefits should be included in the pages for share schemes.

Box 1.23: Expenses payments received

As this is the final box on benefits you may not think it is important. But all employees who have **expense accounts** or get expenses for things like entertainment or travelling **may** have to fill it in.

If your employer has a dispensation for 1997/98 you may not have to fill in any of the expenses boxes (1.23 as well as **1.32–1.35)**. If your employer has a dispensation, you should not have any of these figures on your P11D unless they are expenses that are taxable such as if your employer pays for your home telephone bill.

Expenses dispensations: what every employee should know

In some cases expenses will **not** be listed on your P11D because your employer has agreed a special *dispensation* with the Inland Revenue. This dispensation covers expenses that you can claim back because they are incurred doing your job. As there is no benefit to you (you do not gain because all your expenses are legitimately incurred in doing your job) they are not classed as a benefit for tax purposes. **This dispensation means that you do not have to include these expenses on your Tax Return.** The only figures for expenses you will see on your P11D are the ones on which you must pay tax. If no expenses are included on your P11D do **not** fill in the expenses box.

The whole point of a dispensation is to save paperwork. If your employer does not have a dispensation you must add up all the expenses you receive and write the figure in the expenses box **1.23**. So that you are not taxed on these expenses as though they were a perk of your job, you then have to add up all the expenses that were legitimately incurred on business and claim them as a deduction in boxes **1.32 to 1.35.** In most cases the two figures will be the same and will cancel each other out.

In some cases the Inland Revenue agrees with your employer that minor benefits and expenses can be settled through PAYE – so you may find these included on your Tax Code. But you must still include them on your Tax Return.

Box 1.23:

If your employer does **not** have a dispensation you will have to fill in the box – in this case all expenses should be listed on your P11D. If you want to work out the figure yourself you may need a separate sheet of paper to write down the amount of each type of expense and you must then total these up and put the final figure in box **1.23**. Alternatively, use the form on page E6 of *How to Fill in Your Tax Return* (the leaflet that comes with your Tax Return).

- *Travelling and subsistence payments*. This will include fares, hotels, meals (you can claim these back in box **1.32**) and travel between home and your normal place of work. **Do not** include any expenses or payments for company car or van expenses or expenses towards your own car.
- *Entertainment*. Put in the total amount you receive – this includes any allowances specifically for entertaining.
- *General expenses allowances*. Again put in the amount of the allowance. So if you get a set allowance for expenses regardless of what you spend on company business, you will need to include this.

Do not forget to **total** up all these figures **before** writing the final figure in box **1.23**.

Tax tip: Remember, if any of the expenses in box **1.23** were incurred wholly, exclusively and necessarily for your work, you can claim them back as a deduction in boxes **1.32 to 1.35**.

Balancing charges are to tax you for money you have previously claimed as a *capital allowance*. See box **1.35** on page 127 for details on how this is calculated.

12

REDUNDANCY, LUMP-SUM AND COMPENSATION PAYMENTS

PAPERWORK

- ❑ Details of any redundancy payment you received during the tax year.
- ❑ Details of payments made because you could not continue your job due to injury or disability.
- ❑ Details of payments made from unapproved retirement schemes (most company pension schemes are approved).
- ❑ Help Sheet IR204.

• £30,000 exemption	1.24	£
• Foreign service and disability	1.25	£
• Retirement and death lump sums	1.26	£

Reliefs are tax-free lump sums (one-off cash payments) or the part of a lump sum that is tax free.

Please note, you must read page EN6 and the Notes and fill in Help Sheet IR204 before filling in boxes 1.24 to 1.30.

Box 1.24: The £30,000 redundancy exemption

When you are made *redundant*, the first £30,000 of payment you receive is tax free (provided it meets certain criteria) and anything over this is taxed in the normal way through PAYE. Redundancy will include redundancy payments under an Inland Revenue approved or government scheme, pay in lieu of notice and other payments provided they are not for work done.

When you are made redundant, normal wages, pay in lieu of holiday, pay for working your notice period and commission are usually taxed as usual under PAYE and are **not** tax free. Lump sums that you received in the April 1997 to April 1998 tax year that related to a termination of employment **before** the tax year do not have to be included (but you should tell your Tax Office as these should be included in your tax calculation for the earlier year).

Certain redundancy payments are **not** tax free:

- payments made as a term of condition of your employment (it is written into your contract that you will receive a certain payoff);
- payments for work already done;
- payments for undertakings not to take another job (golden handcuffs or restrictive covenants).

Enter in box **1.24** the total amount of redundancy that is tax free. If you received **more** than £30,000, put the figure £30,000 in this box. If you received less than £30,000, put the amount of qualifying redundancy you received.

Then in box **1.29** put the amount of redundancy received over the £30,000 threshold and any redundancy payments that are taxable. If you have more than one taxable lump sum you will have to add the figures together before entering the total in this box.

Make sure you include any tax deducted in box **1.30**.

Box 1.25: Foreign service and disability

Only include the payments, or the part of the payment, that is tax free. Foreign service covers payments made to you when you were made redundant or received compensation for loss of a job entirely or substantially outside the UK and are tax free if:

- 75 per cent of your total service was foreign service; or
- the last ten years out of 20 were foreign service; or
- in a total service of more than 20 years, 50 per cent was foreign.

You can claim a partial exemption for some foreign service that does not meet these requirements. See Help Sheet IR204.

Disability covers payments made to you if you could no longer do your job because of injury or disability (accidents are covered in the next box). This payment is tax free.

Box 1.26: Retirement and death lump sums

This box only covers payments from or payments into unapproved retirement benefit schemes. **Your company pension is normally 'approved' so you will not have to worry about filling this box**. Money your employer pays into a retirement benefit scheme or uses to buy you an annuity (under certain conditions) and certain lump sums from your employer's pension scheme are also tax free.

A few pension schemes are non-approved by the Inland Revenue. These are often 'top-up' schemes for executives who want to boost their pension but have exceeded the limit they are allowed to pay into their approved company pension scheme. Some payments from non-approved pension schemes are tax free and do not have to be included in box **1.28**. They are:

- ❑ payment on retirement or death as a result of accident;
- ❑ if the lump sum was funded by contributions you made (you have paid tax on these already);
- ❑ or funded by contributions from your employer upon which you have already paid tax (these schemes are known as funded unapproved retirement benefit schemes or FURBs).

TAXABLE LUMP SUMS

Box 1.27

- From box H of *Help Sheet IR204* — 1.27 £
- From box Q of *Help Sheet IR204* — 1.28 £
- From box R of *Help Sheet IR204* — 1.29 £

Include any taxable lump sums including:

- ❑ redundancy and termination payments received under the terms and conditions of your contract (where your contract states you will get a set lump sum for a certain amount of service or when a job ends);

- 'golden handcuffs' or payments made to you on condition you will not take certain actions such as taking on another job (also known as restrictive covenants);
- bonuses on leaving a job.

Box 1.28:

Put here any taxable amounts for payments listed in box **1.26**.

Box 1.29:

Put remaining lump sums that are taxable including payments for the termination of foreign service that are not exempt or only partially exempt. You should also include the proportion of redundancy payments that are **not** tax free and included in box **1.24**.

Box 1.30

Write the amount of tax deducted already from items listed in **1.27** to **1.29**. So if you have been made redundant, the payment over £30,000 will normally have been taxed already under PAYE – enter the tax deducted or you will pay it twice.

> **Tax tip:** If you get pay in lieu of notice it is normally tax free. But if the company you work for goes into liquidation or bankruptcy you will be paid with basic-rate tax deducted from the whole amount. If this tax is more than the tax you would have paid if it had been taxed as normal pay, you can get a tax refund. Do not fill this in the lump-sum section, but in the earnings box **1.10** and write an explanation in the 'Additional information' box on page 8 of your Tax Return.

Box 1.31: Foreign earnings not taxable in the UK

You will normally only have to fill this box in if you ticked the non-residence box on page 2 of your core Tax Return. Notes on page E6 of your Tax Return Guide explain this in more detail. This box is important as the figure you enter will be deducted from your income before it is taxed (ie it will reduce your tax bill).

13

ALLOWABLE EMPLOYEE EXPENSES

Boxes 1.32 to 1.36: How to make sure you are not taxed on business expenses

• Travel and subsistence costs	1.32 £
• Fixed deductions for expenses	1.33 £
• Professional fees and subscriptions	1.34 £
• Other expenses and capital allowances	1.35 £
• Tick box 1.36 if the figure in box 1.32 includes travelling from home to work	1.36

You **do not have to fill these boxes in if your employer has a dispensation**. You will know if there is **no** dispensation as the full amount of expenses you received will be included on form P11D and you would have had to fill in box **1.23**.

These boxes allow you to claim back expenses listed in box **1.23**. The reason why you have to fill in these boxes is to make sure you are not taxed on expenses as a perk.

If you use your own car for business use you should fill in this section to claim back the costs of running your car.

You can **only** list expenses that are necessary travelling expenses and related meal and accommodation costs **incurred in doing your job** and other **necessary** expenses incurred **solely** in doing your job. They must either have been included as expenses received in box **1.23** or have been paid by you but **not** claimed back from your employer.

If you have more than one item to include in this box you will have to add up the total.

Box 1.32: Travel and subsistence costs

You can include business journeys – but not journeys to and from your normal place of work. However, you will in some cases be able to claim expenses for journeys to a temporary place of work (see notes on page E7 of the Revenue guide on how to fill in your Tax Return). If you are a travelling salesmen or travel as an integral part of your job you can claim the costs incurred from the point you left home. You can also claim for meals while you are on a business journey. You can claim back incidental expenses of £5 for every night spent away from home (newspapers, telephone calls home, etc) but **no** other personal expenses.

> **Tax warning:** From April 1998 new rules have come into force covering travel and subsistence payments. Only travel expenses after deducting the normal cost of travelling from home to work are tax deductible. Once this has been deducted from your expenses you may be left out of pocket. It means you will be required to keep more detailed records. Your employer should have notified you about these.

If your employer pays certain costs for repairing, insuring and taxing your company car direct (i.e. you do not pay the costs and reclaim them on expenses) it does not affect your tax position. However, if you reclaim these costs on expenses – and these expenses are listed in box **1.23** – you can reclaim the proportion attributable to your business mileage in box **1.32**.

Fill in this box if your mileage allowance is less than that you are allowed to claim without paying tax. See Table 11.1 on mileage allowances on page 110 for an explanation of how to calculate this figure.

If you make a claim for mileage allowance in this box you will **not** be able to claim a *capital allowance* to help cover the costs of buying your car (in box **1.35**). You can only claim one or the other.

Box 1.33: Fixed deductions:

You should be aware of these as they are agreements made by your trade union or worker representative body agreeing a fixed amount for costs that those in your type of work incur. This could be for replacing tools or buying special working clothes. If you want to claim these costs but not under a fixed deduction, include the costs in box **1.35**.

Box 1.34: Professional fees and subscriptions:

These are also tax deductible if you have to join a professional body in order to carry out your profession. Ask your professional body for advice on whether your subscriptions are allowable and how much you can deduct.

Box 1.35: Other expenses and capital allowances:

Claim any expenses you incurred **necessarily** and **solely** in doing your work. 'Necessarily' means the costs everyone doing your job would have to meet and which have to be incurred in doing your job.

Also include the business proportion of benefits included in full in box **1.22**, director's and employee's liability insurance, the cost of upkeep of tools and special clothing and any other expense not covered in boxes **1.32** to **1.34**.

The *capital allowances* you can claim are for the cost of equipment or machinery you use in your employment – the allowance covers the cost of depreciation of assets or equipment which you have to provide for use in carrying out your job. Generally you can only claim for items necessary for you to carry out your duties – for example office equipment – but you can also include **private cars used for business** provided you have **not** already claimed for running costs under the mileage allowance.

To qualify for a capital allowance, the items must have a useful life of at least two years and must be things which every person doing your job would have to provide. However, the most common item to come into this category is a private car used for business. If you have bought any other equipment ask for the Help Sheet IR203.

The *capital allowance* you can deduct on cars is 25 per cent of the cost of the car, and in subsequent years a further 25 per cent of the balance.

So, if the car costs £12,000:

Year 1 capital allowance is 25% of £12,000 = **£3000** (put this figure in box **1.35**).

Year 2 you can claim a capital allowance on the remaining balance:

£12,000 – £3000 (which you have already claimed) = **£9000** (the written-down value).

Year 2 capital allowance 25% of £9000 = **£2250.**

This writing down continues until the car is worthless, sold or you no longer use it for business. The maximum allowance in a year is £3000, and you can only claim the proportion attributed to business. So if 1000 of your 10,000 total miles were on business, you can only claim one-tenth of the capital allowance. This is known as the *business proportion*. You will have to keep detailed records of mileage to prove this. When you sell the car, if the amount you sell it for exceeds the written-down value you will have to pay tax on the difference. This is known as a *balancing charge* and it is taxed in box **1.23**.

Tax tip: You can also get tax relief on interest-paid loans you take out to buy a car which you use in your employer's business and on which you can claim capital allowances. The interest relief can be claimed in the first four years of the loan. Again relief is restricted to business use of the vehicle. You should claim this in box **1.32** along with other costs of running and maintaining your car.

Box 1.36:

The cost of travel from home to work is not allowed as a deductible expense and as such the Inland Revenue will want to know if you have included this in your expenses boxes on page E1.

Box 1.37: Foreign earnings deduction

Write the amount of earnings you received while working abroad during the 'qualifying period' of 365 days or more (with no single visits of more than 62 consecutive days). This will ensure you are not taxed on these earnings. Ask for Help Sheet 205. There are special rules for seafarers.

Box 1.38: Foreign tax relief

There are two ways to ensure you do not pay tax on foreign earnings in both the UK and the country where you worked. First, you can deduct any tax paid on your foreign earnings. Second, you can claim tax credit relief. If you want to claim back the tax, fill in the amount here. But you may find that you are better off claiming a tax credit. If you want the tax credit, leave the book blank. See Chapter 18 in Part 4.

> **Tip:** If you think any of the information you have supplied needs further explanation, write the details in the 'Additional information' box at the end of the employment pages.

If you did not tick any other boxes on page 2 of your Tax Return you can now go back to ***STEP 2*** and tick the box that states you have filled in your supplementary pages. Then go straight to Part 4 of this book for details on how to fill in the rest of your Tax Return.

PART 4

A GUIDE TO FILLING IN THE OTHER SUPPLEMENTARY PAGES

As this book is primarily aimed at employees (Kogan Page publishes a separate book for the self-employed), pensioners and those in receipt of investment income, few readers of this book will need to fill in any of the supplementary pages of the Tax Return. As such, the following sections are not covered in such great depth. However, those who do need to fill in any of these pages will find that, while step-by-step guidance on filling in each box has been cut back, the amount of tax advice and tax tips are still covered in great detail.

Note: Even if you do not have to fill in any of the supplementary pages, you may find the tax-saving tips useful.

14

SHARE SCHEMES

Only fill in these pages if you ticked the Share scheme box on page 2 of your core tax return.

> **Important:** These pages only cover Income Tax due – Capital Gains Tax (the tax on the profit you make when you sell shares) is covered on a separate part of your Tax Return. Profits on the sale of shares are taxable because once you own the shares they are no longer in the tax-free scheme.

Dividends from shares received through an employee share scheme (the dividends you earn after you have converted your savings into shares) should **not** be included here. Include them on page 3 of your Tax Return.

Many share schemes are tax exempt – so you may not have to fill in any of the boxes even though you received shares from a share scheme during the tax year.

Note: Share options are schemes giving employees an *option* to buy shares in the company for which they work at a later date and usually at a favourable price.

The following should **not** be included in the Share scheme pages:

- ❑ **Approved profit-sharing schemes*.** These give a yearly tax-free allocation of shares to employees. Shares are only taxed if they are kept in the Scheme Trust for less than three years (five years for periods up to 28 April 1996). If these shares are taxable, PAYE will normally be deducted. Your employer or the trustees of the profit-sharing scheme will tell you how much has been paid to you and how much tax has been deducted so you can include the figures in your employee payments box **1.10** and your employee tax deducted box **1.11** on your Employment form.

- ❑ **Save As You Earn (SAYE) schemes.** These are also known as **approved savings-related share option scheme**s and are run by your employer. You will have been offered the chance to buy shares at a discount. This is a share option. The shares can be at a discount of up to 20 per cent lower than the stock market value on the date your option is granted. You can save up to £250 a month to buy these shares and after five or seven years (depending on the scheme contract) buy the shares or take your savings. The only tax you may have to pay is Capital Gains Tax when you sell the shares.

  These schemes are tax free and you **do not** have to fill in these pages provided:
  - you have **not** taken your shares (*exercised your option*) within three years of being granted the share option;
  - you have **not** bought your shares within three years because your company was taken over; and
  - your scheme is approved* by the Inland Revenue.
- ❑ **Approved* executive share option schemes**. These are now known as discretionary share option schemes. From 17 July 1995 shares can no longer be offered to you at a discount. Whether or not you have to pay tax depends on the date you were granted the options. If it was on or before 17 July 1995 you **do not** have to pay tax or fill in these pages provided:
  - the scheme is approved*;
  - the option is exercised no sooner than three years after it is granted and within ten years, and;
  - at least three years after any previous options were exercised.

If you were granted the options after 17 July 1995 there is an additional requirement. These are only are tax free provided the total value of all shares granted to you was £30,000 or less at the time new options were granted (although some schemes were covered by transitional provisions until 31 December 1996).

***Note:** 'approved' means approved as a tax-free scheme by the Inland Revenue.

If you are in an unapproved scheme you will pay Income Tax on the difference between the market value you pay when you buy your shares (exercise the option) and the amount (if any) you paid for the option. The market value is not the stock market closing price but an agreed value between your employer and the Shares Valuation Division of the Inland Revenue. Ask your employer if you are uncertain of the value to use.

Tax tips:

- If you are offered the chance to take up share options or invest in a savings-related share option scheme (SAYE scheme) make sure you meet the requirements above so that you do not pay tax.
- When you take your shares out of a share scheme, you will then be liable for tax on any dividends and could be liable for Capital Gains Tax on any subsequent increase in the share price. To avoid this, transfer them into a single-company personal equity plan (PEP). You must do this within 90 days. However, this tax break will not be available for much longer as these schemes are being abolished from April 1999.
- If you are a member of a savings-related SAYE scheme, remember that you do not have to take (or *exercise*) your share options. If the price of the shares falls to below the price you can buy the shares for (the *option price*) you can take the cash instead. Your money will have been invested and earned a competitive rate of interest and this is tax free.
- If you benefit from an executive, or approved, discretionary share option scheme, make sure you keep records of when you were granted and exercised any share options as you cannot take them within three years or after ten years. And if you take shares you cannot exercise any more options for three years without paying tax.

PAPERWORK REQUIRED

You will need a separate page S2 (the second page) for each Share scheme 'event' that is taxable. An *event* is every time you *exercised* an option (bought shares) or an option was *granted* (you were given the option to buy shares at a later date). You will need to have your share option certificate, copy of any exercise notice, any correspondence or other explanatory information received from your employer about the share transaction and information on the market value of the shares at the relevant dates.

Before you can fill in the form you need to know if the shares were *unquoted* – this simply means they were not quoted (or listed) on the Stock Exchange or the Unlisted Securities Market (USM). Tick the unquoted boxes if the shares were not listed on the Stock Exchange.

SHARE OPTIONS

Page S1:

This only has to be filled in once – regardless of how many share options you exercise. If you have shares in more than one company, list one name in box **2.1** and the others in the 'Additional information' box at the bottom of the page.

Boxes 2.1 to 2.6:
Approved savings-related share options:

	Name of company	Tick if shares unlisted	Taxable amount
• Exercise	2.1	2.2	2.3 £
• Cancellation or release	2.4	2.5	2.6 £

You probably know these as Save As You Earn schemes. However, you **only** have to fill these boxes in if the share options are taxable (the criteria are explained earlier in this chapter). To work out the taxable value fill in boxes **2.32** to **2.41** on page S2.

If you have been given money for giving up the option or for not exercising it (for instance when your company was taken over) this is classed as a *cancellation or release,* so fill in that column rather than the exercise column. Cancellation or release also covers receiving something for transferring, cancelling, realizing or not exercising your option.

Boxes 2.6 to 2.12:
Approved discretionary share options:

	Name of company		
• Exercise	2.7	2.8	2.9 £
• Cancellation or release	2.10	2.11	2.12 £

You will not have to fill in these boxes if your share scheme met the criteria listed at the beginning of this chapter.

If your options are taxable, you will pay tax on the difference between the market value of the shares at the time you exercised the option and the amount paid for the shares. If you have already filled in box **2.32** because you also have a savings-related scheme, you will need to fill in a separate form. Then fill in the exercise column on page S2.

Boxes 2.13 to 2.21: Unapproved share options

	Name of company		
• Grant	2.13	2.14	2.15 £
• Exercise	2.16	2.17	2.18 £
• Cancellation or release	2.19	2.20	2.21 £

These are schemes not approved by the Inland Revenue that are therefore taxable. This box should **also** be filled in if you were granted an option in an *approved discretionary share option* scheme where the option price (the price you can buy the shares for) is **less** than the market value of the shares at the date the option was granted to you.

Unapproved share options may be taxed on **both** the grant of the share option **and** the exercise of a share option.

Boxes 2.22 to 2.30: Shares as employee benefits

Shares you get as a result of your employment are treated as an employment benefit for tax purposes. You need to fill in the shares acquired section if, because of your employment, you were able to buy shares or an interest in shares for **less** than they were worth at the time or you were given them for **free**.

You do **not** have to fill in the section if you were given a priority allocation of shares when your company was floated on the Stock Market or a public offer for shares was made provided you paid the same price as members of the public.

Tax tip: If you have bought shares in a close company which has a closed or limited number of shareholders, and you were a shareholder with more than 5 per cent or worked in running the business, you can claim tax relief on interest paid on actual loans to buy shares. The same applies if you buy shares in an employee-controlled company. See Help Sheet IR216.

Boxes 2.28: Post acquisition charges

This taxes you for the increased value of cheaper free shares bought in your company under the 'Shares received from your employment' and 'Shares as benefits' sections and also for any benefits you received because you owned the shares (such as if you gain a further right to dividends). See Help Sheet IR217 for a full explanation and how to work out the figures.

15

SELF-EMPLOYMENT

This chapter is aimed primarily at those who have a small amount of earnings from self-employed or freelance earnings in addition to their main salary, who:

- do not have an accountant;
- want to know what information to give their accountant or tax agent;
- want a better understanding of how they are taxed; and
- want to know what they can deduct to reduce their overall tax bill.

Kogan Page publishes a book specifically aimed at the self-employed which will be of greater use to those with larger amounts of earnings from self-employment.

Note: The Inland Revenue has special rules to help those whose profits are irregular and may have self-employed earnings one year and none the next. If you are an author or artist, a farmer or market gardener, a foster carer or adult carer, ask the Inland Revenue for the special rules that will help you to even out your tax bill.

PAPERWORK

One copy of the Self-employment pages for each set of business accounts. These are the accounts drawn up at the end of your accounting year. If you don't have accounts drawn up, you will need records of income and expenditure. If you pay tax 'on account' (in two instalments) you should have been sent a 'Self Assessment –

Statement of Account' form – a tax bill sent for payment by 31 January 1998. You will need this, and the notice of the second instalment in July, to calculate how much tax you still owe for the 1997/98 tax year.

Note: This chapter refers to your business. You may not consider yourself to be 'in business' because your earnings are low, occasional or in addition to earnings from employment. But from the point of view of the Inland Revenue, you are 'in business'.

WHAT IF I ONLY RECEIVE OCCASIONAL, SMALL OR PART-TIME EARNINGS?

If you are an employee who earns extra money from freelance or consultancy work, this is classed as self-employment. Remember, you can be an employee **and** self-employed. And you can be self-employed on a part-time or spare-time basis. Although you may not think that you are running your own business, for tax purposes you are. Only if you receive very isolated payments can you avoid filling in the self-employment pages. If this is the case you can put these additional earnings in the 'other income' box on page 4 of your Tax Return.

If you are unsure as to whether or not you are self-employed you must generally:

- ❑ work for more than one person or employer;
- ❑ pick the hours you work;
- ❑ provide your own tools and equipment;
- ❑ operate your own business structure – invoicing, business bank account, etc.;
- ❑ determine what work you do and how you carry it out;
- ❑ take financial risks – investing your own money in your business.

'The badges of trade' which determine that you are trading rather than investing or doing something as a hobby are:

- ❑ **Frequency or number of similar transactions by the same person.** You buy and sell similar items with the aim of making a profit and do so frequently – for instance, you buy and sell a lot of antiques.

- ❑ **Buying and selling within a short period of time.** You sell items which you haven't owned for very long.
- ❑ **Supplementary work.** You alter or improve items so you can make more when you sell them – for instance, you restore classic cars and then sell them on for a profit on a frequent basis. Supplementary work also includes money and time spent on advertising.
- ❑ **Motive.** Your motive for buying and selling is to make a profit.
- ❑ **Subject matter of the sale.** If you sell something that you bought for your own use or benefit then you are not trading. But if you sell things that you bought with the aim of making a profit you could be classed as self-employed.

WHAT YOU NEED TO KNOW TO FILL IN THESE PAGES

Your *accounting date* is the date up to which you draw up your accounts. It is the end of your *accounting year*, which is usually a 12-month period. If you only have a small amount of self-employment or freelance earnings you may have simply opted to be taxed over the same period as the tax year itself – from 6 April to 5 April. This is known as being taxed on an *actual basis*. The *accounting year* you must use is the one ending in the 1997/98 tax year. So if your accounting year ends on 5 May 1997 you will include profits for the 12 months to 5 May 1997 on your 1997/98 Tax Return – and then pay this tax by 31 January 1999. Please note that all the self-employed are now taxed on a *current year* basis. Under the old *preceding year* basis you were taxed on your accounting year ending in the previous tax year.

Special rules for those with new businesses or who closed a business during the tax year

When you set up in business or close a business you are not necessarily taxed on your accounting year. Read the Tax Guidance notes to find out over what period you will be taxed. These rules mean you could be taxed on the same profits twice – these are known as *overlap profits*. You can claim these back when your business ceases to trade or, in some cases, if you change your accounting year.

Tax tips:

- If you have made a loss during the first four tax years of your business, you can offset the loss against income (including salary) you earned in the three tax years before the year in which the loss was made. But to do this you must make a claim by 31 January, 22 months after the year in which you made the loss.
- If you spent money on setting up your business before you actually started trading you can also claim pre-trading expenses. So money you spend on rent and rates or business equipment can be tax deducted from your business profits after you start trading. The expenses can be incurred up to seven years before your business actually starts.

IF YOU DO NOT HAVE ACCOUNTS DRAWN UP

You no longer need to send your statement of accounts in with your Tax Return. However, you will still need to have accounts to fill in your Tax Return. So it may pay you to employ an accountant to do this – **accountancy fees are tax deductible.**

However, you can draw up your own accounts if your turnover is low, you don't employ staff and you know what is required – your accounts must meet accepted accountancy standards.

Remember your turnover should include the value of sales you have made in the accounting year including invoices you have sent out for services or goods provided – even if you have not yet been paid.

You don't need to have a balance sheet to fill in your Tax Return but if your business involves keeping stock you may find this useful.

HOW TO FILL IN THE SELF-EMPLOYMENT TAX PAGES

If you want to explain any figures or clarify a point, use the 'Additional information' boxes on your Self-employment form. Your notes may answer any questions the Tax Office may have and save them having to write to you or make an enquiry into your accounts.

Boxes 3.1 to 3.5: Business details

Name of business
3.1

Description of business
3.2

Address of business
3.3

Postcode

Accounting period -

Start
3.4 / /

End
3.5 / /

Enter the name of your business – if you do not have a business name enter your own name in box 3.1, a brief description of your trade (for example builder) in box 3.2 and your trading address (or home address if you work from home in box 3.3). Tick in box **3.6** if any of these details have changed since your last Tax Return.

If you have more than one business you **must** complete boxes **3.1** to **3.3** on a separate set of self-employment pages for each business.

Write the accounting period for which you are providing details of income and expenses in boxes **3.4** and **3.5**. Read the notes on page SEN2 of your Tax Return guide before filling in any of the remaining boxes. They will only normally apply if you have changed accounting dates. And then fill in any dates such as starting or closing date of your business or a change in accounting date.

Boxes 3.11 to 3.13: Income and expenses for businesses with a turnover below £15,000

- Turnover, other business receipts and goods etc. taken for personal use — 3.11 £
- Expenses allowable for tax — 3.12 £

box 3.11 *minus* box 3.12

Net profit (put figure in brackets if a loss) — 3.13 £

Because this book is aimed at those with only a small amount of earnings from self-employment it assumes that these are the boxes you need to fill in. If your annual turnover is more than this (remember if you have been trading for less than a year you must increase your turnover proportionately) you must fill in page SE2.

If you have a statement of accounts, use the figures that are included on that – then fill in the three boxes and go to page SE3.

If your *annual turnover* is less than £15,000 and you have **more than one business** you **must** complete a set of Self-employment pages for each business.

Box 3.11: Turnover

Your turnover must include sales and other business receipts and:

- ❑ include the normal selling price of any goods you have taken for personal use or for your family or friends (the difference between any price paid for the goods and the normal selling price should go in box **3.54**);
- ❑ include income which has been earned but not received (if someone is late in paying or you think they will not pay you can make a provision for doubtful debts but can only tax deduct bad debts written off). Note even if you have not issued an invoice, you will usually be treated as earning the income at the time the goods or services are provided;
- ❑ do not include interest received from your bank or building society (put that on your main Tax Return with other savings income);
- ❑ do not include any capital allowances or balancing charges – these cover capital assets such as buildings, machinery, cars, computers. These are included on page SE3;
- ❑ do not include Enterprise Allowance or Business Start Up Allowance (these go in box **3.88**).

Box 3.12: Expenses

It is essential that you deduct every expense allowed to reduce your taxable profits. That is why you are required to keep accurate and detailed records of all expenditure – and if you do not you could be fined up to £3000.

WHAT YOU CAN DEDUCT TO REDUCE YOUR TAX BILL

Generally you can deduct any expense that is incurred *wholly and exclusively* for the purpose of the business you run. Employees must also show that these expenses are *necessarily* incurred. So as a self-employed person you have more freedom to deduct expenses from your income to reduce your profits – and in turn your tax bill. You don't have to prove they were necessary and even the wholly and exclusively rule has exceptions – you can claim for your car if you use it for both personal and business use.

This makes expenses easier to justify. Basically you can **deduct most expenses and expenditure which form part of your day-to-day running costs, apart from:**

- ❑ anything you buy for personal use;
- ❑ items bought for domestic use;
- ❑ capital items such as business premises, equipment and any expenditure incurred with such items, for example the legal expense of acquiring them (these capital items are tax deductible – but under capital allowances);
- ❑ anything not prohibited, eg entertainment expenses;
- ❑ anything you can deduct under another tax provision, eg deeds of covenants; and
- ❑ **not** your own wages.

If an item is not used wholly and exclusively you can only claim a proportion of it against tax – the portion you use for business. For instance, you may use your car for both business and private purposes. So you will only be able to claim the proportion of car expenses which is attributable to business use. You can work this out on a mileage basis. So if half your mileage is for business you should be able to deduct half your car expenses.

A list of what you are and are not allowed to deduct is given on page SE5 of the Inland Revenue notes on self-employment. An additional list is given on Help Sheet IR221 (which you should request if you don't already have it).

Do not forget to claim the 'cost of sales', the cost of buying raw materials to make your goods or provide your service and stock you buy for resale. You can only normally claim for the costs of goods and raw materials used to make items actually sold. However, you can deduct the costs of raw materials that are part way through manufacturing and costs incurred in large service contracts as *work-in-progress* costs. If you sell stock you must do your stocktaking at the end of the year and work out how much of your stock was actually sold.

There are special taxation rules for the construction industry. Ask your Tax Office for advice.

Tax tips:

- If your spouse, partner or a family member helps you to run your business, pay them a wage and you can then tax deduct this as a business expense. But work must actually be done – you cannot just give them the money. But be careful not to pay them more than £62 a week (the 1997/98 threshold) as you will then have to deduct and pay National Insurance as an employer. Check with your Tax Office that you will not have to deduct tax under PAYE.
- If you make a payment that covers an expense for more than one accounting period (for instance 12 months of rent) only deduct the proportion that relates to the accounting period on your Tax Return.
- If you are not registered for VAT you can claim back any VAT paid on your expenses.

Expenses that can be claimed by those working from home

Running a business from home has major advantages. For a start, you do not have the additional costs of renting business premises and you can keep your overheads to a minimum. You can also claim some of the costs of running your home to reduce your tax bill.

You can only deduct a proportion of the running costs of the home that relate to work. So if you have five rooms in your home excluding kitchens and bathrooms and use one room exclusively for work or business, you can deduct a fifth of the running costs. If you do not use a room exclusively for business you will have to estimate a figure and agree this with your Tax Office.

You can generally claim the business proportion of:

- rent or mortgage interest;
- heating, lighting and telephone bills;
- insurance costs; and
- cleaning costs.

Do not forget to claim capital allowances for any office equipment such as tables/desks and chairs (see page SE3).

Tax warning: If you use your home for business and deduct part of the running costs as a business expense, you may have to pay capital gains tax on the profits made when you sell the property. To get round this rule, never use part of your home exclusively for business – only mainly for business.

Box 3.13: Profit/loss:

Your profit or loss is your income minus your expenses. If you made a loss write that figure in brackets.

IF YOUR BUSINESS MAKES A LOSS

You can offset losses to reduce your tax liability in either the same year as you made the loss or in other accounting years. You can claim tax relief for your losses by making a deduction from:

- your income for the year. This includes investment income and **earnings from employment;**
- your capital gains;
- your business profits taxed in earlier years; or
- by carrying forward your losses to offset against future profits.

Tax tip: If you are an employee and make a loss on your freelance earnings, you can offset these losses to reduce the tax you pay on your salary. However, you cannot set up a business purely to make a loss and reduce the tax you pay on other sources of income.

The Tax Return advises you to go straight to page SE3. However, if you have drawn up your own accounts and are worried that you may have left something out, take a photocopy of page SE2 and work through boxes **3.16** to **3.52.**

Tax tip: Read through the notes for page SE2 as you may find that you have forgotten to deduct an expense or have wrongly deducted something that is not allowed.

	total of boxes 3.17 to 3.32
• Disallowable expenses	3.53 £
• Goods etc. taken for personal use and other adjustments (apart from disallowable expenses) that increase profits	3.54 £

TAX ADJUSTMENTS TO NET PROFIT OR LOSS

Only fill in this part of the Tax Return if you have filled in boxes 3.14 to 3.52. To ensure you have not made a mistake on page SE1, here is what some of the boxes mean.

Box 3.53: Disallowable expenses:

If you have included any disallowable expenses such as entertaining in the expenses box, these should be deducted as they are not tax deductible.

Box 3.54: Goods taken out of the business

If you included the price you paid for goods taken out for personal use (or for friends and family) in your turnover, deduct the amount paid for the goods before writing in the normal selling price of all goods taken out for such use. Total up boxes **3.53** and **3.54** and put the figure in box **3.55**.

Box 3.536: Deductions from net profits:

This covers an assortment of extras that are included elsewhere on your Tax Return such as bank interest (so they do not need to be taxed again under self-employment) and taxes you have already paid (you will not want to be taxed twice).

CAPITAL ALLOWANCES

You cannot deduct every item of expenditure as an allowable business expense. Items of capital investment known as capital expenditure must be deducted separately as a *capital allowance* even though they will be deducted from your business profits before calculating how much tax you need to pay.

Capital allowances are given at 25 per cent (but at 50 per cent this year – see tax tips on page 151) on items of equipment, plant and machinery including furniture, computers, tools and cars. Industrial buildings (not shops, business premises or retail outlets), hotels and agricultural buildings get a reduced allowance of 4 per cent.

You can only usually get capital allowances on items used *wholly and exclusively* for the business and that belong to the business. But you can claim a proportion of the costs for some items, such as cars that are for part business and part private use.

Capital allowances cover those items that have a useful life of more than two or three years. So spending on computer software will be an allowable business expense (100 per cent tax deductible) rather than a capital allowance (25 per cent tax deductible in the first year) unless you buy the software as a package with your computer.

Tax tips:

- ❑ If you buy equipment for private use (such as a computer or desk) and then use it in your business, you can claim a capital allowance on its market value at the time you start using it for business.
- ❑ If you buy on hire purchase, you can claim capital allowances on the original cost of the item (the part you pay as a down payment). The extra amount you pay in interest or other charges can be claimed as a business expense.

HOW TO WORK OUT YOUR CAPITAL ALLOWANCES

For plant and machinery, computers, etc. you can claim up to **25 per cent** of the cost in the year in which you buy it. The rest is written off over a number of years at up to 25 per cent of the remaining value. For example:

> You spend **£3000** on a computer.
>
> *Year 1:* In the year you bought it you can deduct 25 per cent as a capital allowance = **£750**
>
> It now has a *written-down* value of £3000 – £750 = **£2250**
>
> *Year 2:* In the second year you can claim a capital allowance of 25 per cent on this written down value of £2250:
>
> 25 per cent of £2250 = **£562.50**
>
> The written down value is now £2250 – £562.50 = **£1687.50**
>
> *Following years:* You continue writing down your asset until it is completely written off, you no longer use the item or you sell it.

To make things more simple you can put all your plant and machinery into a *pool of expenditure* so you do not have to calculate each item separately. You take the written down value of all items in each pool (the different pools are listed on your Tax Return) and deduct 25 per cent (or the rate that applies to that pool).

Cars, but not lorries and vans, must be calculated separately or in their own pool if you have purchased more than one. The maximum you can write down for any car in any year is £3000. Cars which cost more than £12,000 cannot be included in this pool and must be calculated separately, as must **cars used partly for private motoring.**

Also note that *short-life* assets, those with a useful life of four years or less, must be calculated separately and not included in the general pool.

When you sell your asset, give it away or it ceases to be of any use, a separate calculation must be made. The *balancing charge* taxes you for any profit you make from selling an asset for more than the amount you have deducted from your tax bill (the written-down value). The *balancing allowance* compensates you for any losses – if you sell an asset for less than the written-down value. If you give an asset away you must calculate this figure using the market value.

Warning: If you are a new business and your accounting period is not 12 months you must either reduce or increase your allowances proportionately. So if you have only been in business for six months you can only claim half the capital allowance.

Tax tips:

- Because of the way capital allowances work, it may be more tax efficient to lease an item of equipment as you can claim 100 per cent of the leasing costs as a business expense but only 25 per cent as a capital allowance.
- A special tax break is given to small and medium sizes business (those with a turnover of £11.2 million) this year. **Any capital expenditure between 2 July 1997 and 1 July 1998 will qualify for a 50 per cent first-year allowance.** This means you can deduct 50 per cent of the costs in the first year, reducing to 25 per cent of the written-down value thereafter. Note that it does not matter when you incurred the expenditure during the tax year. Even if you buy an asset at the end of your accounting period you can deduct the entire 50 per cent. Only if your accounting period is less than 12 months will you have to reduce the allowance proportionately.

ADJUSTMENTS TO ARRIVE AT TAXABLE PROFIT OR LOSS

Boxes 3.71 to 3.88:

Use this section to: adjust your profits by either adding any balancing charges or deducting any capital allowances; to offset your losses against other income; *carry forward* losses to offset against future profits; or *carry back* losses to get a tax rebate on taxable profits in past years.

Add in any other business income from Enterprise Allowance or Business Start Up Allowance and any other amounts not included elsewhere in the Self-employment pages and include them in box **3.87**. A note in the 'Additional information' box on page 4 of the Self-employment pages will prevent the Tax Office asking about this. Then calculate your total taxable profits from this business.

Read the notes in your Revenue Tax Return guide before filling in boxes 3.71 to 3.78.

CLASS 4 NATIONAL INSURANCE CONTRIBUTIONS

These payments are collected by the Inland Revenue because they are based on the profits you make from your trade or profession. Note that you can no longer claim half your contributions against tax.

You do not have to pay Class 4 contributions if:

- ❑ your profits are below the lower profits limit listed in Table 15.1 on page 153;

> **Tax tip:** If you are both employed and self-employed you may not have to pay Class 4 National Insurance contributions. If you already pay the annual maximum of National Insurance contributions, which is **£2160** (which you will if you are an employee **and** earned £465 or more a week in the 1997/98 tax year) you should ask the Department of Social Security for a deferral. If you cannot claim a deferral in advance, Class 4 National Insurance will be deducted from your self-employment earnings and you will then have to claim a repayment.

- ❑ you were a man aged over 65 or a woman aged over 60 at 6 April 1997;
- ❑ you were aged under 16 at 6 April 1997 (provided you have been granted an exception by the Contributions Agency).

If you don't have to pay Class 4 National Insurance contributions or you have asked for a deferment tick box **3.89** and put a '0' in box **3.91**. Give an explanation as to why you do not need to pay National Insurance in the 'Additional information' box.

If you run more than one business you should also make sure that you do not pay more than the maximum. Ask for Help Sheet IR220.

Box 3.90

You can offset losses from earlier years (if they have not already been used) to reduce profits chargeable to National Insurance. You can also deduct interest earned on savings or bank balances from your profits as you do not pay National Insurance on non-trading income.

Box 3.91

Work out the National Insurance you owe using the figures in the box below.

If you don't want to calculate the amount of National Insurance you have to pay, the Tax Office will do this for you. Leave the box **3.92** blank.

Table 15.1 gives the National Insurance rates you must pay on profits and the thresholds at which they become payable. This table does not cover Class 2 contributions that are paid by the self-employed at a flat rate.

National Insurance contributions are only paid on profits above the lower threshold and you do not pay any contributions on earnings above the upper threshold. So the maximum Class 4 National Insurance contributions paid by the self-employed in 1997/98 will be: £24,180 – £7010 = £17,170 (amount between the lower and upper limits) x 6% = **£1030**.

Table 15.1 *National Insurance rates for the self-employed*

Self-Employed Class 4 Contributions	**1997/1998**
Lower profits limit (per year) – no NI contributions payable on profits and gains below this limit	£7010.00
Upper profits limit (per year) – no NI contributions payable on profits and gains above this limit	£24,180.00
Rate of all contributions payable	6%

Box 3.92:

This relates to the construction industry only, and only to subcontractors who have had tax deducted at source.

Boxes 3.93 to 3.109: Summary of Balance Sheet

You only need to fill this in if you have a balance sheet. This section is not used to calculate your tax bill.

Additional information

Explain any figures or accounting decisions here. This may answer questions that your Tax Office has to ask you and prevent an inspector mounting an investigation into your accounts.

16

PARTNERSHIPS

You must fill in the Partnership pages of your Tax Return if – at any time during the 1997/98 tax year – you earned a share of profits, losses or income from a business which you carried out in partnership. This also covers income, profits and losses that you were entitled to – so even if you took no money out of the partnership you must still fill in the pages.

There are two types of Partnership pages to fill in:

- The short version is for those whose only partnership income was
  - a share of trading or professional income;
  - interest with tax deducted from banks, building societies or deposit takers.
- The long or full version which covers all possible types of partnership income.

Which of these you fill in will not only depend on what type of income you receive but also on the *partnership statement* you receive.

This chapter deals with the short version as that is the one most readers will receive.

You will need separate Partnership pages for each partnership you are in and for each business the partnership carries on.

HOW TAX ON PARTNERSHIPS HAS CHANGED

Partners are now:

- taxed on the individual partner not the partnership;
- taxed on a current-year basis.

From 31 January 1998 all partners had to make their first tax payment as an individual partner paying their first instalment or *payment on account* for the 1997/98 tax year. There is no longer a tax assessment on the partnership. You are now also taxed on a current-year basis which means you must include any profits for the accounting year ending in the April 1997 to April 1998 tax year on this tax return. In the past some partnerships (those set up before 6 April 1994) were taxed on a preceding year basis which meant they were taxed on the accounting year ending in the previous tax year.

Note: When you join or leave a partnership, legally one partnership comes to and end and another begins even though the business carries on uninterrupted. To avoid this, a partnership can elect for a *continuation*. This means that the business continues to be treated as though it had carried on as usual. Only if the business ceases to trade does the partnership come to an end.

PAPERWORK

Your will need your Partnership returns and accounts, the Inland Revenue notes on Partnerships and any relevant Help Sheets listed at the beginning of the Inland Revenue notes. Filling in the forms is much easier than for the self-employed as you can rely on your Partnership accounts for much of the information.

TIPS FOR FILLING IN YOUR PARTNERSHIP TAX PAGES

Most of the information can be copied from your partnership accounts. Remember you are only taxed on your share of partnership profits (as determined by your partnership agreement). As with profits from self-employment, you can offset losses against other income (such as income from employment) in the 1997/98 tax year or carry back losses to offset against partnership profits from a previous year or carry them forward to offset against future profits.

See the notes in Chapter 15 on self-employment for other tax tips as the same rules apply to partners as to the self-employed.

17

LAND AND PROPERTY

These pages have to be filled in by anyone who received income from land and property in the tax year – even if this rent is tax free under the tax-free Rent a Room scheme.

However, if you received income from renting out a holiday home **overseas** this should not be included here but on the Foreign pages.

If you received income from land and property that was owned by a partnership, that income should be included in the Partnership pages.

Land and property also includes rents from immobile caravans and permanent houseboats.

PAPERWORK

It is essential for you to keep accurate and detailed records if you are to make the most of the expenses you can deduct from your income to reduce your tax bill. Make sure you have all your accounts to hand, records of rent received and any bills relating to the rented property or land. These should include:

- ❑ rent, rates, insurance, ground rents, service charges, etc;
- ❑ any bills for repairs and maintenance;
- ❑ your mortgage interest statements or other loan details;
- ❑ any bills you have for legal, accountancy, surveying and other costs;
- ❑ details of any wages you have paid out.

Warning: Before starting to fill in these pages make sure your accounts cover the same period as the tax year. If they do not, you will have to recalculate them so you only include income and expenses received and incurred during the tax year.

THE RENT A ROOM SCHEME

This is the scheme that allows you to rent out a room in your home and receive up to £4250 a year – or almost £82 a week – tax free.

The tax break only applies if the room is furnished, is in your only or main home and you do not let rooms for a business (such as a guest house).

You can only rent out **one** room. You cannot try to claim two lots of allowance by getting someone else in your home to rent out a second room. If two rooms are let in the same property, one by you and one by someone you own the property with, the allowance is halved to £2125.

If you receive £4250 or less from renting out a room, tick the ***YES*** box on the top of the Land and Property page. There is no point in taking up the option of working out your profit as all of this rental income is tax free.

If you earn **more** than £4250 in rent you can **either** claim the Rent a Room allowance and pay tax on the amount of rent over this limit **or** be taxed on your rental profits. Your rental profits will be the amount you receive in rent minus expenses. In most cases you will be better off claiming the rent-a room allowance. Only work out the rental profits if your expenses are more than £4250. See the 'other property income' section of this chapter for a list of the types of expenses you can deduct.

Tax tip: If your home is jointly owned, look at the tax advantages of splitting your Rent a Room allowance if your rent **exceeds** the £4250 limit. If your spouse, or whoever else jointly owns your home, pays tax at a lower rate you will be better off splitting the rent so half of it is taxed at a lower rate.

FURNISHED HOLIDAY LETTINGS

To qualify as furnished holiday lettings, the property must be:

- ❑ furnished;
- ❑ available for holiday letting to the public at a commercial rent for 140 days or more during the year;
- ❑ actually let commercially as holiday accommodation for 70 days or more during the year; and
- ❑ not occupied continuously for more than 31 days by the same person for at least seven months of the year.

See page L2 of your tax notes for further details.

If you rent out an immovable caravan this is also classed as a furnished holiday letting provided it meets the above criteria.

If you own and let holiday property with another or other people, only include your share of rent and your share of expenses.

Tax tip: If your holiday letting nearly fits these criteria, make sure it does next year. There are tax advantages. For a start, if you make any losses you can use these to reduce your tax bill on earnings from employment or profits from self-employment. You cannot do this with other rental income, you can only use losses to offset against tax on other property profits. Furnished holiday lettings have other tax advantages. You can claim capital allowances (a proportion of the amount you spend) on furniture, fixtures and fittings. With other types of rental income you can only claim for *wear and tear* of these items or the cost of replacing them. But you cannot claim capital allowances **and** replacement costs – only one or the other.

You do not have to itemize expenses or fill in boxes **5.2** to **5.7** if your rental income is less than £15,000 a year. Just fill in the total amount claimed. A full list of what can be deducted is included in the 'other property income' section of this chapter.

Tax tip: If you let more than one furnished holiday home you can average out the days the properties are let so you can pass the 70-day rule.

Note: If you buy anything for your rented property that is also partly for private use you should put the **total** amount spent in the expenses boxes and then deduct the value of the proportion that was for private use in box **5.10**.

> **Tax tip:** furnished holiday lettings are the only type of rental you can use to offset losses against other income **and** capital gains. You can even use losses in this year **to reduce your tax bill in an earlier year**.

OTHER PROPERTY INCOME

This covers all property income other than furnished holiday lettings and the Rent a Room scheme (unless you want to opt out of this and be taxed on rental profits in the usual way). This broad category includes everything from leasing out acres of land to renting your property out to a film crew.

Do **not** include income from Enterprise Zone trusts. These go on page 3 of your main Tax Return.

Remember the rent is classed as being received when you earned it, **not** when you actually get paid. If you have a bad debt that you cannot recover reasonably you can deduct this. And if you are paid in advance for rent and some of this relates to the period after 5 April 1998, this does not have to be included. You cannot evade tax by taking payment in kind – for instance you are given the free use of a car or other goods or services.

If your income is from the granting of a lease see page L5 of your notes for special rules.

EXPENSES

Do not itemize these if your total property income is less than £15,000 annually. But you will still need to know what are allowable expenses.

You **cannot** deduct the cost of buying the land or property or the cost of machinery, furnishings or furniture or any losses you make when you sell the land or property.

But you can deduct:

- ❑ any rent you pay to someone else for the use of the land or property;
- ❑ council tax, business rates, ground rents;
- ❑ heat and light (gas and electricity);
- ❑ insurance against loss of rent;
- ❑ insurance of the property;
- ❑ maintenance and repairs from painting to roof repairs (but not a new roof) and damp course repairs (but not any improvements);
- ❑ **interest on a loan to buy your property** and any costs incurred in arranging the loan;
- ❑ legal and professional costs of letting a property for a **year or less**;
- ❑ **accountancy fees for drawing up your accounts;**
- ❑ the costs of evicting a tenant;
- ❑ management expenses as a landlord – telephone calls, stationery, travelling for business purposes;
- ❑ advertising, estate agent and accommodation agency fees;
- ❑ **either** *wear and tear*: you cannot claim the purchase costs of equipment or furniture in a let residential property (unless it is a furnished holiday let) as an allowable expense, however, you can claim 10 per cent of the rent (after deducting service charges and water rates) for wear and tear of fixtures, fittings, cookers, even lampshades, beds and sheets;

  or *replacement and renewal*: this allows you to claim the full cost of replacing furniture, furnishings and household equipment – but only when you need to replace them.

  You have to choose between renewal expenses and wear and tear – you cannot have both and once you have chosen a basis you must stick to it.

You cannot claim for:

- ❑ the costs of your own time;
- ❑ the costs of buying the property (only loan interest);
- ❑ the costs of improving the property (this is deducted as a cost when you sell the property and reduces your Capital Gains Tax liability).

Make sure you keep all receipts so you can tax deduct every expense incurred *wholly and exclusively* for the purpose of your rental business. This will include light bulbs, toilet rolls and cleaning fluids.

Tax tips:

- If you are considering buying a home for letting you may be better off taking out a loan as interest payments are tax deductible and you do not have to tie up your capital.
- If it is your only or main home that you are renting out (say while you are working overseas) you may still be able to claim MIRAS – mortgage interest tax relief at source – which gives you 15 per cent tax relief on interest payments made on the first £30,000 of your home loan. Alternatively you can claim all the interest as an allowable expense and opt out of MIRAS. This will give you a bigger saving unless your rents are very low. Ask your Tax Office for advice.
- You can also claim wages paid to gardeners, porters, cleaners, etc. Consider employing your spouse if he or she is a non-taxpayer and does not earn enough to pay National Insurance (pay is less than £62 a week for the 1997/98 tax year). This way you can pay the wage free of tax and save the hassle of calculating PAYE and National Insurance. But remember, work must actually be done.

Boxes 5.11 and 5.12 and 5.33 and 5.36:

Capital allowances enable you to tax deduct some of the purchase price of items you use in letting your property. **These cannot include furniture or household equipment unless the property is classed as a furnished holiday let.** However, if the property is **not** a furnished home (it is a commercial property) you can claim capital allowances on furniture, fixtures and fittings.

All landlords can deduct the cost of any machinery or equipment used in maintaining the property such as ladders, tools and even garden equipment such as lawnmowers. You can also claim for the cost of constructing agricultural buildings, industrial and commercial buildings in Enterprise Zones and certain types of hotel. See Chapter 15 on self-employment for guidance on how to work out capital allowances.

Tax tip: If an item that was previously for private use is now used in your business you can claim a capital allowance on its market value when you start using it for business.

If you only use items partly for business or want to know any more about capital allowances, ask for Help Sheet IR250. If you want to claim agricultural buildings allowance, ask for Help Sheet IR224.

TAX ADJUSTMENTS

As from 6 April 1995 all property you let is treated as one type of business and all income and expenses are aggregated (added up together) so you can offset one type of property loss against another (other than losses on overseas properties). Only losses from furnished holiday lets can be offset against other types of income (for instance income from employment or self-employment).

However, all rental losses can be *carried forward*. This means you can use your losses this year to reduce your profits from rental income in future years.

Agricultural estates or land managed as one estate are treated differently. Ask for Help Sheet IR 251.

Tax warning: When you sell a property that has been let out you may have to pay Capital Gains Tax on the profit. This will also be charged if you let part of your main home. See Chapter 20 on Capital Gains Tax.

18

FOREIGN INCOME

Do not confuse this with Non-residence. Foreign covers income from overseas, Non-residence is for those who live overseas.

This chapter covers savings that are in overseas or offshore accounts, dividends from overseas shares, offshore investment funds, overseas pensions and social security benefits and any income you receive from land and property including overseas holiday homes that you let out.

PAPERWORK

You will need any dividend vouchers, bank statements, pensions advice notes, foreign tax assessment and receipts for foreign tax paid. If you invest in an overseas unit trust or investment fund you will need your fund voucher (although note that if you invest in a UK unit or investment trust that in turn invests in overseas shares this should be included on page 3 of your main Tax Return). If you have a property overseas you will also need to have all your receipts for expenses – from the cost of your mortgage to maintenance and caretaking bills. The guidance notes from the Inland Revenue (which you should ask for if you have not received them) are 22 pages long but only because each country has a different tax arrangement (or Treaty) with the UK and these are listed in full.

You will need a calculator to help you convert all income into sterling.

These pages will also enable you to reclaim any foreign Income Tax deducted from your overseas income. You can also reclaim Capital Gains Tax paid in a foreign country. You can use this to reduce (offset) some of your UK bill. You can calculate the tax credit yourself by following Part B of the notes provided by the Inland Revenue.

However, this chapter does not deal with profits made on the sale of overseas homes or offshore and overseas shares and investments. You must include these on the Capital Gains pages.

Note: All foreign income is now taxed on a current year basis which means you pay tax on income earned during the 1997/98 tax year. In past years you paid tax on the preceding year basis which means – had the rules not changed – you would have included income for 1996/97 on your 1997/98 Tax Return.

> **Tax warning:** You will be taxed on your foreign income as you earn it, not on the date you bring the money into the UK or are paid it. However, if exchange controls mean you cannot bring the income into the UK it should not be taxable.

All amounts must be listed in sterling and you must use the exchange rate on the day you earned the foreign income (not received it or brought it into the UK). Working out what exchange rate to use can be difficult. Ask your Tax Office for help.

If you are resident in the UK but not domiciled here for tax purposes or are a citizen of the Commonwealth or the Republic of Ireland, special rules apply. These are the remittance basis rules and cover income you receive in the UK. Ask for the Non-residence pages by ringing the Orderline on 0645 000 404 and read the notes carefully.

If your savings and investments are in *joint names,* only enter your share of the income.

> **Tax warning:** You can only reclaim foreign tax at the official rates agreed. There is a full list in your Inland Revenue guidance notes.

HOW TO CLAIM BACK FOREIGN TAX

If tax has been deducted from your foreign income by an overseas tax authority you can claim back the tax in one of two ways:

- by deducting it from the amount of income and gains which will be taxed in the UK (put this final figure in box E on the Tax Return); or
- by claiming tax credit relief.

This second option is normally the best. However, if the foreign tax is higher than the UK tax you can only claim *tax credit relief* up to the amount of UK tax you will pay. This tax credit will reduce your tax but only on the same income – it cannot be used to reduce tax on other types of income.

These rules ensure that you are not taxed twice. However, if you are not liable to UK income tax you cannot claim the extra foreign tax back by using the tax credit system.

If your foreign income is paid to you through a UK agent (eg a bank) tax will already be deducted. The agent should allow for any double taxation agreement.

FOREIGN SAVINGS

These include savings, interest and dividends but **not** offshore unit and investment trusts or other offshore funds.

Foreign income dividends (FIDS) from UK companies should be included on page 3 of your main Tax Return.

Each block of shares and each savings account is a separate source of income and should be listed separately. Shares bought at different times are also separate entries.

Ignore the unremittable box **unless** you are not domiciled in the UK for tax purposes but live in the UK **or** if you are a citizen of the Commonwealth or Republic of Ireland **and** are resident in the UK.

If you receive dividends from Finland, France, Italy or the Republic of Ireland you may be able to get the other country's tax credit in addition to any dividend. Add this tax credit to the dividend to get the figure to put in box B.

Tax tips:

- ❑ You cannot claim tax credit relief on dividends paid in some countries including Cyprus, Malta, Jersey and the Isle of Man. But you can deduct the tax charged when calculating the amount of dividend on which you have to pay UK tax.
- ❑ If you hold savings accounts in joint names you can elect to have a larger share apportioned to the partner who pays tax at the lowest rate.
- ❑ You can get foreign tax reduced or claim another country's tax credit (for instance on tax dividends) by writing to the Financial Intermediaries and Claims Office (International), Fitzroy House, PO Box 46, Nottingham, BG2 1BD or telephoning them on 0115-974 2000.

OVERSEAS PENSIONS AND BENEFITS

Some pensions and social security benefits are exempt from UK tax. Read page F7 of your Inland Revenue notes. Also note that only 90 per cent of the pension income from an overseas employer scheme or pension fund is taxed.

Remember if you are **not** claiming a foreign tax credit, deduct any foreign tax from your total pension or benefit (the figure in box B) and write this figure in column E.

INCOME FROM LAND AND PROPERTY ABROAD

You must fill in the relevant section of page F2 (boxes A to E) **and** page F4. On page F2 leave column C blank. You will need a separate F2 for each property.

If, in a rare case, your rental income accounts are drawn up for a year that is not the same as the tax year, ask your Tax Office for advice. Only rent received or due in the tax year must be included on your Tax Return.

Read the Land and Property chapter for details of what you can deduct as expenses. Do **not** itemize expenses if your total income in the year before expenses is **less than £15,000.** If the property is leasehold you can claim for any rents you pay under the lease (or part of these rents if your home is only let out for part of the year.) If you pay for caretakers and cleaners, overseas property agents and gardeners, claim for these along with advertising costs. You will find it difficult to claim the cost of air fares unless you can prove that the travel was *wholly and exclusively* for the purposes of the overseas letting business

Tax tip: You can deduct from your rental income interest you pay on a loan to buy the property abroad (something that was not available before 6 April 1995).

Tax warning: If you or your family use your overseas home for part of the year and rent it out for the remainder you must apportion your costs accordingly. The same applies if you only rent out part of the property.

OFFSHORE FUNDS

If you have invested in an offshore unit trust where income is automatically reinvested (rollover funds) you still have to declare this income. The unit trust company should give you a tax voucher showing if foreign tax was deducted.

Some distributor funds have equalization arrangements, which means that part of your income may actually be a refund of capital. Check your redemption voucher to make sure you do not pay tax on anything you should not.

FOREIGN LIFE INSURANCE POLICIES

Income and gains from most offshore insurance policies do not usually have foreign tax deducted but if it is deducted you **cannot** claim it as a tax credit relief and you cannot use it to reduce your gains in box **6.8.** This is because life insurance policies are treated as though basic-rate tax is deducted. You only have to pay extra tax if you are a higher-rate taxpayer.

> **Tax tip:** Qualifying offshore life insurance polices do not give rise to taxable capital gains. These have to be a minimum of ten-year policies and must be approved by the Inland Revenue.

FOREIGN TAX CREDITS

Page F3 is for you to total up the tax credits you are claiming for foreign tax deducted on income in other sections of your Tax Return including:

- employment;
- self-employment;
- partnerships; or
- capital gains.

You can only claim tax credit relief if you have included the tax in the income or turnover figures you have entered elsewhere. If you have deducted foreign tax before writing in your income, you cannot claim a tax credit as well.

19

TRUSTS

Trusts are a specialist area of tax. However, you do not have to know about trust law as the trust deed will have been drafted by a solicitor. You only have to know how much income you received from a trust. In this case you are the *beneficiary*.

You will also have to fill in this form if you are a *settlor.* This means you have set up a trust fund.

This chapter does not deal with unit or investment trusts. They should be included on your main Tax Return on page 3.

PAPERWORK

All documentation given to you by the trustee of your trust. If you have received money from an estate of a deceased person you should have a statement of the amounts paid from the estate by the personal representative who is administering the estate. All you have to do is copy this information onto the Trust page. If you are entitled to income from a trust by right (it is not a discretionary trust) you can ask your trustees for a Certificate of Income and Tax Deduction (Form R185E) which will detail the figures you need.

Before filling in the page you will need to know if the income you received is taxable and if it should be included on this page or another part of your Tax Return.

INTEREST IN POSSESSION TRUSTS

The term *absolute right to income* means that you get that income automatically. It is not at the discretion of trustees. These include life interest trusts/interest in possession trusts.

Because you have an automatic right to the income, for tax purposes, the trust is disregarded. As such you must **not** include certain income on the Trusts page.

Include in section 10 of your main Tax Return:

- share dividends from UK companies;
- dividends from UK authorized unit trusts;
- dividends from investment trusts (open-ended investment companies).

Include on the Foreign pages:

- all foreign interest and dividends.

TAXATION OF DISCRETIONARY AND ACCUMULATION TRUSTS

Discretionary trusts (when payments are made at the discretion of the trustees) and accumulation trusts (usually set up to avoid or reduce inheritance tax and to pass wealth onto future generations aged under 25 when the trust is set up) are taxed at 34 per cent.

> **Tax tip:** If you are a basic 23 per cent taxpayer, you can reclaim some of the 34 per cent tax on your trust (34 per cent − 23 per cent = 11 per cent). Unless you pay 40 per cent tax you will be entitled to a tax rebate.

The representative administering the trust should tell you what to include on your Tax Return. Enter in box **7.3** the total gross income (without tax deducted), put the tax deducted (the amount of tax deducted at 34 per cent) in box **7.2** and the amount you actually received in box **7.1**.

If tax has been deducted at the lower 20 per cent rate (or you have a tax credit at that rate) fill in boxes **7.4** to **7.6**. Tax is deducted at the lower rate on share dividends and building society saving interest.

Settlors – those who set up trusts – may also have to declare their income in boxes **7.1** to **7.6**. This will be if you retain an interest in the trust. This simply means that the money could be paid to you in **any** circumstances whatsoever (however remote the possibility). This could be from the beneficiary dying and the capital being returned to you **or** the trust deeds being written in such a way that you or your spouse could become beneficiaries.

Tax warning: You will also have to declare income if you make a settlement in favour of children under 16 as any income that is paid to them from a trust you set up is classed as being for your benefit. However, this will exclude gross (without tax deducted) income of £100 or less a year.

Tax tip: To get round these rules you can get the grandparents to set up the trust.

Because these rules are so wide-ranging, if you are a settlor you should ask for Help Sheet IR270 by ringing the Orderline on 0645 000 404.

INCOME FROM THE ESTATES OF DECEASED PERSONS

This does not include income earned on inheritances and legacies after they are paid to you. Any income earned on these inheritances **after** you receive them should be included on the relevant section of your Tax Return – for instance, savings interest should be included on P3.

This section does include income earned after a person has deceased and while the estate is being managed but **before** you are paid any inheritance. For instance, the estate may earn interest or rental income from a property – this income should be declared in boxes **7.7** to **7.18**.

Fill in the relevant boxes:

- ❑ Basic rate means 23 per cent tax has been deducted.
- ❑ Lower rate means 20 per cent has been deducted – for instance, from savings interest or share dividends.
- ❑ Non-repayable means tax has been deducted and you cannot reclaim this tax – for instance, income earned from a life insurance investment.

20

CAPITAL GAINS

In addition to Income Tax, Capital Gains Tax is the other major tax that is assessed through your Tax Return. These two taxes cover most of the money you are likely to receive – one taxes your income and the other your profits.

You pay Capital Gains Tax if you sell or *dispose* of an *asset* – a possession, investment or business – and you receive *capital* – a sum of cash – and have made a *gain* – or a profit. You pay the tax on the profit you make, **not** on the amount you receive when you sell the asset.

There is a much higher allowance (the amount you can earn before tax) than for Income Tax. And it is a tax that is fairly simple to avoid. As a result only 75,000 taxpayers actually pay the tax each year.

You are required to fill in the Capital Gains Tax pages if you have made profits (gains) on the sale of assets (investments, second homes, shares, antiques, inheritances) and:

- ❑ these total more than £13,000 (not each); or
- ❑ you have made profits of more than £6500; or
- ❑ you have sold your main home and you have used this for running a business or have rented it out; and
- ❑ although the tax form does not stipulate this, you should also fill in the Capital Gains Tax pages if you made **losses from the sale of assets.** You can then use these to reduce your tax bill – in this year, or past or future years.

Even if you fall into one of these categories you may still **not** have to pay Capital Gains Tax. Some items are exempt and others will not be taxable because you can reduce your profits by deducting expenses and inflation.

PAPERWORK

It is essential for you to keep accurate and detailed records in order to make sure you are filling in the right figures. You will have a major problem if you have not kept receipts or statements showing when you bought each item, how much you paid, any costs involved in the purchase, any expenditure to improve the item and how much you sold it for.

You will also need a calculator as you have to do all the calculations yourself; you will probably have to do these on a separate piece of paper.

ASSETS LIABLE TO CAPITAL GAINS TAX

- ❑ Shares.
- ❑ Land (apart from the grounds of your main home if they are sold with the property and do not exceed half a hectare).
- ❑ Second homes.
- ❑ Antiques and works of art.
- ❑ Unit and investments trusts.
- ❑ Jewellery and silver (unless they are chattels).
- ❑ Most things you hold for personal or investment purposes – basically any asset that is not exempt.

ASSETS EXEMPT FROM CAPITAL GAINS TAX

These include:

- ❑ private cars;
- ❑ your main home (principal private residence) provided you have not let it out or used it for business;
- ❑ personal possessions or chattels with a predicted useful life of 50 years or less when you get them;
- ❑ Personal Equity Plans (PEPs);
- ❑ bonuses from TESSA accounts;
- ❑ gilts – UK government stocks and some corporate bonds bought after 13 March 1984;
- ❑ shares issued under the enterprise investment scheme;
- ❑ British money including post-1837 gold sovereigns;

- foreign currency for personal use;
- betting and lottery winnings;
- life insurance policies (with some exceptions – mainly short-term policies and those bought from a third party, not the life insurance company);
- National Savings Investments;
- venture capital trusts;
- qualifying corporate bonds (but not on a company share reorganization or takeover);
- personal injury compensation;
- damages including those for defamation or personal injury;
- decorations for valour that belong to your family (your grandfather's George Cross);
- gifts to charities and certain national institutions;
- trading stock you sell (if you are running a business);
- money you get as a gift or on money (or an asset) which is taxable as part of your income – or which would be subject to Income Tax.
- inheritances – when you die there is no capital gains on your estate, but Inheritance Tax may be charged. However, when you sell an inheritance you may be liable to Capital Gains Tax on any profits you have made while you have owned the inheritance.

Tax tips:

- To avoid the risk of having to pay capital gains tax on the sale of shares – including shares from a SAYE company share scheme – invest using a Personal Equity Plan (PEP). You can invest up to £3000 a year in a single-share PEP and can transfer shares worth up to this amount from profit-sharing schemes and approved savings-related share option (SAYE) schemes. But note that PEPs will be abolished from April 1999.
- Whenever possible you should try to use up your Capital Gains Tax Allowance. You can no longer do this by using a tax avoidance system known as *bed and breakfasting* which enables you to sell shares, unit or investment trusts at the end of the tax year to use up your Capital Gains Tax allowance and then buy the same assets back the next day.

HOW DO I KNOW IF I HAVE MADE A GAIN?

You make a gain if the value of something you sold has risen in value since you bought it (or since 31 March 1982 if you want to use this date). You do not pay tax on the first £6500 of gains (this limit is for the sale of **all** assets) and you only pay tax on gains above this limit. You will pay Capital Gains Tax at your top rate of tax.

You may make a capital gain even if you do not sell an asset – for instance if you give it away, exchange it or sell the rights to it or you get insurance money if it is lost or destroyed. If you do not sell the asset, the market value of the asset at the time of disposal is taken as its value when calculating Capital Gains Tax. The date you dispose of an asset is the date that you must use when calculating your profit – not necessarily the date you are paid.

To work out if you have made a gain you must calculate the profit. Take the price you sold the asset for and deduct:

- ❑ the price you paid for the asset or its value at the time it was given to you;
- ❑ costs incurred in buying and selling – including valuer's/surveyor's fees, auction fees, the cost of legal advice, stamp duty, advertising costs, stockbroking fees (if you only sell part of an asset, such as part of a block of shares, you can only claim a proportion of the costs);
- ❑ costs of enhancing the value of the asset – restoration etc;
- ❑ inflation (see your tax return guide for the amount you can deduct).

You cannot deduct:

- ❑ interest you paid on a loan used to buy the asset.

Tax tips:

- ❑ If you held/owned the asset on **31 March 1982** you can elect to substitute its market value on that date instead of the actual cost. This is known as *rebasing*. So any appreciation/profit you made before that date will not be taxed. However, it you opt for this, you **cannot** include any expenses incurred before 31 March 1982. Once you have elected for rebasing this will cover **all** your assets and you cannot change your mind. But if you have **not** made such an election you can treat each asset differently. Also work out gains from the original purchase date to see if your gains will be lower. In this case you can also claim expenses incurred before 31 March 1982. But indexation (the factor that adjusts your gain to take inflation into account) did not start until March 1982 so you can only deduct the effects of inflation from March 1982 onwards. In some cases one figure (say gains since 1982) will produce a loss and the other (gains since 1970 or whenever you purchased the item) a profit. In this case ask your Tax Officer for advice as you may not have to pay any Capital Gains Tax.

- ❑ If you make a loss on the sale of an asset you must use this to reduce your Capital Gains Tax bill for 1997/98. But you should not reduce the gain to less than £6500 – the Capital Gains Tax threshold. Any additional losses can be offset against other income or capital gains in future years. If your losses reduce your gains to less than £6500, ignore box **8.7** and enter '0' in box **8.8**. If you have any extra or surplus losses you can use these to reduce your capital gains next year or in subsequent years. This is known as *carrying forward* losses.
- ❑ If you have made a loss on shares in a trading company (that is not quoted on the stock exchange) you can offset this loss against your income to **reduce your Income Tax** rather than against your capital gain but only if you subscribed for new shares. You can also claim as a loss anything that was destroyed or no longer has any value (or negligible value) including shares in companies that have gone into liquidation.
- ❑ You can also claim losses from a business against your Capital Gains Tax. And you can use losses from some rented property but only those classed as furnished holiday lettings (see Land and Property). You don't have to use these here, they can also be included in box **13.6** of your main Tax Return.

Tax warning: You cannot claim to have made a capital loss if that loss was created by deducting inflation, known as the *indexation allowance*. The inflation factor can only reduce profits, not create losses. But the indexation allowance can also be applied to costs in buying the assets and costs of enhancing the assets.

CHATTELS AND WASTING ASSETS

If you buy anything that has a predictable life of 50 years or less on the date on which you acquired it, when you sell it you will **not** pay Capital Gains Tax (provided you have not used it in your business and have or could have claimed capital allowances). This can include anything from a racehorse to electronic equipment.

The same applies to 'chattels'. This is a legal term that means an 'item of tangible, moveable property'. This will include items of household furniture, paintings, antiques, items of crockery and china, plate and silverware, private cars, lorries, motor cycles and any equipment or machinery that is not permanently fixed to the building (anything from your washing machine to your computer).

You only have to pay Capital Gains Tax on these chattels if you make a profit of **£6000 per item** and only on the profit over £6000. **Either** calculate the taxable sum by multiplying the profit above £6000 by 5/3 (in this calculation you cannot make any deductions for costs or indexation), **or** you can calculate the *net gain* by taking the total sale proceeds, not just the amount over £6000, and deducting costs as for other assets. After you have done these two calculations you put the **lower** figure in box **8.1**. Note, if you have more than one item you will have to add these up when you fill in page CG2.

If you made a loss you can only claim losses assuming you sold the asset for £6000. If you sold the asset for less than £6000 you must assume you received £6000 from the sale.

> **Tax warning:** You cannot get round this rule by selling a set of items separately to the same person or group of people. So if you have a set of antique chairs you cannot claim each chair as a separate item.

CAPITAL GAINS AND YOUR HOME

Your main home is exempt from Capital Gains Tax when you sell it. This is known as *private residence relief*. But there are some exceptions to this rule, ie if you sold some land, earned money from your home (for instance by renting it out) or used your home for running a business. So if you bought a home and converted into self-contained flats and sold them off you would be liable to Capital Gains Tax. The same applies if you built a second home in your garden.

If the property has been partially **rented**, then you could be liable for tax on the area let for the period of the letting. If it was only let for a few years, you will only pay tax on apropriation of the profits made over the total years of ownership and on the proportion of the home let.

Tax tips:

- ❑ **If you rent out or let your property the gains up to £40,000 are exempt.** So there is no tax to pay.
- ❑ If you have a **lodger** the whole home will qualify for private residence relief. Only if you have more than one lodger could your home become liable to Capital Gains Tax.
- ❑ The final 36 months of ownership of your main home always qualify as tax exempt (for private residence relief) regardless of whether you let the property out during that time.
- ❑ Your home may still be regarded as your principle private residence even if you have not been living in it because you have been employed outside the UK or have been forced to live elsewhere because of your job (but not for more than four years).
- ❑ If you buy a home but cannot move into it because you are unable to sell your existing home you can own both homes for up to 12 months without being liable for Capital Gains Tax.
- ❑ If you work from home – either on a self-employed basis or as an employee – you may be liable to Capital Gains Tax if you use part of your home exclusively for business. To get round, this use a room **almost exclusively** for business. You will still be able to claim for heating, light and your telephone and other expenses.

If you are still unsure about your tax situation, ask for Help Sheet IR282 Private Residence Relief.

CAPITAL GAINS AND MARRIED COUPLES

If you give something to your husband or wife no Capital Gains Tax liability arises on this gift providing you are living together. Remember, if you give an asset away, it is normally treated as though you sold it.

However, if the husband or wife then sells this gift, he or she will have to pay Capital Gains Tax from the date the asset was first purchased – not the date the asset was given to the spouse.

Tax tips:

- You can avoid or reduce a Capital Gains Tax bill by making the most of the allowance given to both the husband and wife. If you make a profit of £13,000 on jointly held assets, by splitting this (putting half on the husband's Tax Return and half on the wife's) you may not have to pay Capital Gains Tax.
- Married couples can also transfer assets to make the most of a lower tax rate paid by one partner. Remember, Capital Gains Tax is charged at your top rate of tax. If you are a 40 per cent taxpayer you will pay 40 per cent Capital Gains Tax. If you transfer the asset to your spouse, he or she may only pay 20 per cent or 23 per cent Capital Gains Tax.
- Transfer assets to your spouse so that you can both use up your £6500 allowance.

Tax warning: If you are about to divorce, part of your settlement may mean you have to transfer assets to your spouse. Transfers between spouses are only exempt if you are still married and living together. Make sure you take account of any potential tax liability when reaching your divorce settlement.

OTHER RELIEFS THAT REDUCE YOUR CAPITAL GAINS TAX BILL

If you make a gift, dispose of a home you have provided for a dependent relative, have sold an asset outside the UK but are unable to transfer the proceeds to the UK or have paid Capital Gains Tax in a foreign country, see page CG14 of your Inland Revenue guidance notes for ways you can reduce your tax bill.

Reinvestment relief can also reduce your tax bill. This applies when you use the gain to invest in an unquoted trading company (or another business if you are self-employed or in partnership). You reduce your gain by the amount of the gain you reinvest.

FILLING IN YOUR CAPITAL GAINS TAX FORM

Page CG2

It is important that you give as much information as possible so that the Tax Office does not have to make further enquiries. If there is not enough space, photocopy the form, ask for an additional Capital Gains Tax page or send a covering letter with your Tax Return.

Include details like the address of the building or description of the property you sold, the name of the company in which you held shares, or the address and type of business you sold.

And in the further information box, explain your figures, what reliefs have been claimed, if you have only sold part of the asset, etc.

Column 7 should be ticked if you want to claim relief from Capital Gains Tax. For instance, if you want rollover relief tick this box and explain the type of relief in column 8.

Once you have totalled up the figures on page CG2 they only need to be copied into the boxes on CG1.

21

NON-RESIDENCE

There are major tax advantages to being taxed elsewhere – in a tax haven or country with much lower tax rates than the UK – and as such the Inland Revenue keeps a careful watch for abuse of the rules.

There are different tax treatments depending on whether you are not resident, or not domiciled in the UK.

As such all the questions on the two pages covering non-residence are about you, your nationality and the amount of time you spend in the UK. No income figures have to be filled in.

Generally, if you earn money overseas you will still be taxed on it in the UK unless you are absent from the UK for an entire tax year. See pages NR9 to NR13 of your Inland Revenue guidance notes for what is taxable and what is not under each tax status.

Because each question on the Non-residence pages is straightforward and relates to your individual circumstances, there is little point in telling you how to fill in the 35 different boxes. However, it will be useful for you to know how your answers will affect the way you are taxed.

THE DEFINITION OF NON-RESIDENCE

The term non-resident generally refers to those who spend less than 183 days in the UK in any tax year and less than 91 days a year over a four-year average (for this Tax Return that will be since 5 April 1994). The advantage of being a non-resident is that you pay UK income tax **only** on your UK earnings and **not** on your worldwide income.

But remember you will have to pay tax in the country where you are living. If the taxes are higher in that country than in the UK you may be better off spending more days a year in the UK and being taxed at

UK tax rates. If the tax rates are lower, spend fewer days in the UK.

If you were not 'present' in the UK during the tax year, you are a non-resident (however, that does not mean you cannot be ordinarily resident). You can be non-resident on a yearly basis – this status does not have to permanent.

However, if you are in the armed forces or diplomatic service or another Crown employee you will be taxed as if you worked in the UK. But any extra allowance paid for working abroad will not be taxable.

If you have only recently left the UK (since 6 April 1997) and were ordinarily resident in the UK in the previous tax year ending 5 April 1997 you **cannot** claim to be a non-resident. Only if you have:

- ❑ spent the last tax year abroad (you left the UK before 6 April 1997);
- ❑ are working full-time in another country;
- ❑ have settled in another country and made it your home; or
- ❑ are intending to live in that country for another three years;

can you now claim to be **non-resident** provided you meet the rules of spending fewer than 183 days in the UK in any one tax year or visiting the UK for fewer than 91 days-a-year over a four-year average. You will count as non-resident from the day after you leave until the day before you come back to live in the UK.

The reason why the Tax Return asks for your nationality is that certain long-term UK residents are still regarded as UK residents even if they leave the UK for occasional residence abroad. These include Commonwealth citizens, British citizens and EEA nationals. So you may have to prove that your departure is more than temporary – usually three years or more – and that you have established a home overseas unless you have spent a complete tax year overseas.

> **Tax warning:** You can be a tax resident in the UK at the same time as living in another country. In this case you will have to make sure you are not taxed twice.

Tax tips:

- ❑ Non-residents may be able to continue to claim the UK personal tax allowance of £4045 against any income subject to UK tax.
- ❑ The rules covering residency relate to entire tax years but if you arrive or leave the UK part way through a tax year, you should still be able to claim full personal allowances (the amount you can earn before paying tax).
- ❑ If you are working overseas and are classed as a non-resident but your wife/husband is still resident in the UK, you can transfer unused married couple's allowance to the UK resident.
- ❑ If you work overseas for 365 days or more you can claim the foreign earnings deduction which means all your earnings are tax free. There is a box on your Employment pages for you to claim this. You can still visit the UK but not for more than a sixth or less than 62 days of the year.
- ❑ If you are a non-resident, transfer investments overseas to an offshore tax haven so that income can be earned free of UK tax. And apply for your bank and building society interest to be paid gross (without tax deducted).
- ❑ If you are non-resident in the UK, make the most of this tax status. Make the most of Capital Gains Tax allowances by selling assets in the years you are overseas.

Different rules apply to those coming to live in the UK. They will be treated as **resident** in the UK for tax purposes if they came to live here before the end of the tax year and either have lived or intend to live here for two years or more or have spent more than 363 days here in the four years ending 5 April 1997.

THE DEFINITION OF ORDINARY RESIDENCE

This is a little more permanent than residence status. Ordinary residence, in another country, applies to those who intend to make – or have made – their home abroad. So this will not usually change from year to year.

If your home is here and you are usually resident in the UK and have been for the last four years, you are ordinarily resident here. To qualify as ordinarily resident elsewhere you must generally be resident there for four years. The same tax rules apply as for non-residence.

THE DEFINITION OF DOMICILE

This implies even more permanence and can have major tax advantages if you choose to live in a country with much lower tax rates than the UK. Generally you will have to buy a property in your new country, make a will under its law, apply for permanent residence (if not nationality), dispose of your UK residence, close UK bank accounts and open ones in your new country. So you have to take major steps to prove that you are a permanent resident in your new country and show that there is no intention to return to live in the UK. Again you are allowed to visit the UK for up to 90 days a year.

If you are domiciled outside the UK you should be taxed on your worldwide income at the tax rate in your new country. However, UK earnings will still be taxed in the UK.

If you come to live in the UK you will be required to fill in a domicile questionnaire (DOM1) to ascertain your domicile.

PART 5

A STEP-BY-STEP GUIDE TO FILLING IN THE REST OF YOUR MAIN TAX RETURN

22

THE REMAINING QUESTIONS

Q17: Have you had a tax refund?

Q17	**Have you already had any 1997-98 tax refunded or set off by your Tax Office or the DSS Benefits Agency?** *Read the notes for box 17.1 on page 26 of your Tax Return Guide*	NO	YES	If yes, enter the amount of the refund in box 17.1. 17.1 £

You will know if you had a refund as you will have been sent a cheque either by your Tax Office or the DSS Benefits Agency. If you have received one, fill in the amount in box **17.1**.

Q18	**Do you want to calculate your tax?**	NO	YES	If yes, do it now and then fill in boxes 18.1 to 18.9. Your Tax Calculation Guide will help.

Q18: Do you want to calculate your own tax?

Remember, calculating your tax bill is optional. You are strongly advised to tick the ***NO*** box. The Inland Revenue will then work out your tax for you. As such you will save on time and effort in completing the complex calculation and reduce the risks of making an error. However, you can **only** tick the ***NO*** box if you complete and return your Tax Return **by 30 September 1998.** If you tick the ***NO*** box you do **not** have to fill in boxes 18.1 to 18.9.

Even if you are employing a tax adviser or accountant to calculate your tax you must tick the ***YES*** box. And if you miss the 30 September 1998 deadline for sending back your Tax Return, you must also tick the ***YES*** box and then work through the complex calculations in your tax calculation guide.

Remember, if you tick the ***YES*** box you **must** then complete the Tax Calculation Guide **and** boxes **18.1** to **18.9**.

If you do want to calculate your own tax see Appendix 1: Calculating Your Own Tax for more details of how to fill in boxes **18.1** to **18.9**.

Q19: Repayments of tax

Q19	**Do you want to claim a repayment if you have paid too much tax?** *(If you tick 'No', I will set any amount you are owed against your next tax bill.)*	NO	YES	If yes, fill in boxes 19.1 to 19.12 as appropriate.

This box simply tells the Inland Revenue that you want to have any tax paid to you (or your accountant or other tax adviser) rather than it being offset against your next tax bill.

You can tick the ***YES*** box even if you are unsure whether or not you are due a tax repayment.

Either tick box **19.1** and leave the rest of ***Q19*** blank – this will be the case if you want the repayment sent to the address on the front of your Tax Return – **or** tick box **19.2** and fill in the rest of the boxes – this will be the case if you want any refund paid directly into your bank or building society account or for the repayment to go to your *agent* (your accountant or tax adviser) or *a nominee* (another person). Write the account details in boxes **19.3** to **19.7**. If you want the refund to go to someone else, write that person's name in box **19.8** and their address in box **19.11**. If this person is your agent, tick box **19.99** and write their reference for you in box **19.10.**

Note: You must sign box ***19.12***. This is so your agent cannot ask for tax refunds to be sent to him or her without your consent.

Q20: Checking your details

Q20	**Are your details on the front of the Tax Return wrong?**	NO	YES	If yes, please make any corrections on the front of the form.

Carefully check the details on the front of the Tax Return. If there are any errors, make your corrections on the front of the form.

Q21: Personal details

Boxes 21.1 and 21.2:

Q21 Please give other personal details in boxes 21.1 to 21.6

Please give a daytime telephone number if convenient. It is often simpler to phone if we need to ask you about your Tax Return.

Your telephone number	21.1	Say if you are single, married, widowed, divorced or separated	21.3
or, if you prefer, your agent's telephone number	21.2	**Date of birth**	21.4 / /

(also give your agent's name and reference in the 'Additional information' box on page 8)

Enter your date of birth if you are self-employed, or you were born before 6 April 1933, or you have ticked the 'Yes' box in Question 14, or you are claiming relief for Venture Capital Trust subscriptions

It is very important that you fill in a daytime telephone number for either you or your tax adviser/accountant. If you give your agent's phone number, write his or her name and reference in the 'Additional information' box on page 8 of your Tax Return. By giving a telephone number you can often speed up the processing of your Tax Return and avoid lengthy correspondence with your Tax Office.

Boxes 21.3 and 21.4:

You must fill in your marital status.

Only fill in your date of birth if:

- ❑ you were born before 6 April 1933 (this is so you can claim higher age-related allowances);
- ❑ you are contributing to a personal pension or retirement annuity plan (you ticked the ***YES*** box in Question 14). This is because the amount you can contribute to a personal pension plan and receive tax relief on is dependent on age;
- ❑ you are claiming relief for venture capital trust subscriptions.

Q22: Other information

Box 22.1: New pensions or benefits:

Tick this box if you expect to receive, or have received, a new pension or social security benefit in the 1998/99 tax year. It will help your Tax Office to get your tax code right in the current tax year.

Boxes 21.5 and 21.6

Enter your first two forenames and your National Insurance number (this may be the same as your tax reference number on the front of your Tax Return).

Box 22.2: Collection of tax:

Employees and those in receipt of company pensions or state benefits usually have small amounts of tax they owe collected through their Tax Code. This means that they do not have to pay a tax demand. However, the maximum that can be collected as additional tax in this way is £1000.

For example, if you are an employee and owe £600 in tax you can have this collected by an adjustment in the amount of tax you pay through PAYE. An additional £50 a month will be taken out of your pay in tax, saving you from having to make a lump-sum payment.

Only tick this box if you do **not** want any taxed owed collected through your Tax Code. Note that if you tick the box and owe tax you will have to pay your outstanding tax as a lump sum instead of over a year.

Box 22.3: Provisional figures:

In some cases you may not be able to get final or accurate figures but have to send back your Tax Return to meet the deadline. If this is the case, you can use your best estimates.

Write in the 'Additional information' box which figures are provisional and what box numbers they relate to. You must state why you could not give the final figures and when you expect to get them.

Tax tips:

- ❑ Don't delay in sending back your Tax Return just because you are missing a couple of figures. If you miss the deadline for sending back your Tax Return you will be fined. Give the most accurate estimate you can, and then write to your Tax Office as soon as you have the final figures.
- ❑ You can amend or 'repair' your Tax Return within 12 months of sending it in. So, if you have made a mistake or have new information you can usually change your Tax Return without penalty (although you may have to pay interest on any outstanding tax that should have been paid earlier).

But you must show that you have taken all reasonable steps to get this information. You cannot simply estimate vast amounts of your Tax Return because you have failed to find the relevant information or have not asked for it.

Box 22.4: Rents paid overseas:

Rents paid overseas should have tax deducted at source (you or the landlord's agent must deduct tax before paying the rent to the overseas landlord), although in some cases you can pay rent without deducting tax if it is agreed by the non-resident landlord and the Inland Revenue. You need to tick this box to ensure that rents are taxed correctly. Do not forget to give the landlord's name and address in the 'Additional information' box.

Box 22.5: Business losses and special rules for literary and artistic income:

This box will only apply if:

- ❑ you are self-employed or in partnership and want relief now for 1998/99 trading losses;
- ❑ have received income from a business that has ceased but want this taxed as income for an earlier year; or
- ❑ have literary or artistic income which you want to spread over two years or more.

If you tick this box, do not forget to write the details in the 'Additional information' box.

THE 'ADDITIONAL INFORMATION' BOX

Make the most of this box. Read through the completed pages of your Tax Return to check if there is anything you want to – or need to – explain, question or bring to the attention of your Tax Office. Alternatively, if you are unsure about a particular box or question, make a note of it here. Also make sure you have provided all the additional information that has been requested.

If you do not have enough room to include all these details you can write extra notes on an additional piece of paper and make a note of this enclosure in this box.

By providing this additional information, you may be able to prevent further investigation or correspondence from the Inland Revenue by answering any questions your Tax Inspector has.

Q23: Declaration

Q23 Declaration

I have filled in and am sending back to you the following pages:

	Tick		Tick		Tick
1 TO 8 OF THIS FORM					
EMPLOYMENT		PARTNERSHIP		TRUSTS ETC	
SHARE SCHEMES		LAND & PROPERTY		CAPITAL GAINS	
SELF-EMPLOYMENT		FOREIGN		NON-RESIDENCE ETC	

Before you send your completed Tax Return back to your Tax Office, you must sign the statement below. If you give false information or conceal any part of your income or chargeable gains, you may be liable to financial penalties and/or you may be prosecuted .

23.1 **The information I have given in this Tax Return is correct and complete to the best of my knowledge and belief.**

Signature Date

If you have signed for someone else, please also:

- state the capacity in which you are signing (for example, as executor or receiver)

23.2

- give the name of the person you are signing for and your name and address in the 'Additional information' box above.

Check you have completed and enclosed all the supplementary pages and then tick the boxes in ***Q23.***

Do not forget to sign the Tax Return. If a tax adviser or accountant is filling in the form for you, they can sign the form instead.

Remember to check your Tax Return carefully as once you have signed it you are legally responsible for its content.

Now photocopy all the pages of your Tax Return and additional documents. If the Inland Revenue needs to contact you, you will need to have a record of what you have included on your Tax Return.

And finally . . . do not forget to pay your tax bill by 31 January 1999. If you are calculating your own tax bill, you can send in a cheque with your completed Tax Return. If the Inland Revenue is calculating your tax bill, it will send you a demand. Do not forget that you could find yourself short of cash in January following the Christmas holiday. Make sure you have set aside enough money to pay your tax bill.

APPENDIX 1

CALCULATING YOUR OWN TAX

PAPERWORK REQUIRED

- ❑ Copies of any Notice of Tax Coding which detail any additional taxes you have paid
- ❑ Details of any payments 'on account' – tax you have already paid in advance for the 1997/98 tax year.
- ❑ A copy of the Inland Revenue Tax Calculation Guide.

If you want to calculate your own tax bill – or have to because you missed the 30 September 1998 deadline for asking the Inland Revenue to do this for you – you should tick the ***YES*** box next to question 18 on page 7 of your Tax Return.

You should have received the green coloured Tax Calculation Guide (Form SA151) with your Tax Return.

But before completing it you should check that you do not need a different calculation guide.

You will need to request a different Tax Calculation Guide if you:

- ❑ have any chargeable gains (must pay Capital Gains Tax) – this will be the case if you have a figure in box **8.8** on the Capital Gains pages;
- ❑ have made any gains on UK and foreign life insurance policies – this will be the case if you have completed boxes **6.8, 12.5** and/or **12.8**;
- ❑ have received lump sum and compensation payments and filled in box **1.29** on the Employment pages (or box **1M.45** if you are a Minister of Religion);

- ❑ received income from the estate of a deceased person with a national basic-rate tax credit of 23 per cent – you will find this in box **7.18**;
- ❑ received a refund of surplus additional voluntary contributions from your pension scheme provider (see box **12.12**).

If you have filled in any of the boxes listed above you **must** request a different Tax Calculation Guide by ringing the Orderline on 0645 000 404 (open seven days a week between 8am and 10pm).

Warning: Do **not** complete the Tax Calculation Guide until you have completed the main Tax Return and all the additional pages. Failure to complete all these forms will result in you miscalculating your tax.

Note: Different rules apply for Ministers of Religion and Lloyd's Underwriters who should take special care to read the notes on page 2 of the Tax Calculation Guide.

The Tax Calculation Guide is very complex so you should work through it with care. Rather than repeating what the guide says, this chapter looks at how you can check that you have completed the guide correctly.

The following calculation provides a more simple way of working out your tax. However, it only covers the main sources of income and does not cover: capital gains (only one per cent of taxpayers pay this); non–MIRAS mortgages; over or under payment of tax in past years; income from abroad that qualifies for double taxation relief; loses you wish to offset against income; trusts; taxable gains on life insurance policies; refunds of surplus AUCs or Class 4 National Insurance for the self-employed.

DOUBLE CHECKING THE FIGURES

STEP 1: Add up all your income from employment (if any)

Remember you have to add in taxable benefits in kind (such as company cars) and make sure you do not include anything that is not taxable such as redundancy payments.

If you do not have a figure in any of the boxes mentioned in this guide, ignore that part of the calculation.

Add up:

Employment income (add up boxes 1.8 to 1.10)		£______
Benefits and expenses (add up boxes 1.12 to 1.23)		+ £______
Taxable lump sums (add up boxes 1.27 and 1.28)		+ £______
TOTAL A	**A**	= **£**______

Add up:

Expenses not taxable (add up boxes 1.32 to 1.35*)		+ £______
TOTAL B	**B**	= **£**______
Now **deduct** B from A to give C	**A − B = C**	= **£**______

Now add up any personal pension plan contributions (you do not need to include payments to company pension schemes):

Employee personal pension contributions (gross) (add up boxes 14.15, 14.16, 14.17)	**D**	£______
Deduct this figure from C to give E	**C − D = E**	£______

STEP 2: Add to this your income from self-employment (if any)

	E	£______
Self employment (box 3.89)		+ £______

* Make sure you do not include any travel from home to work in box 1.32

Now **deduct** any self-employed personal pension contributions			– £_______
TOTAL F		**F**	= £_______

STEP 3: Add this to all other non-savings

		F	**£**
Property income	(box 5.43)		+ £_______
Share schemes	(box 2.31)		+ £_______
Foreign income	(add up boxes 6.2, 6.4 and 6.5)		+ £_______
Pensions and other benefits received	(add up boxes 11.1 to 11.7)		+ £_______
	(add up boxes 11.9 and 11.12)		+ £_______
Maintenance received	(box 12.3)		+ £_______
Other income	(box 13.3)		+ £_______
TOTAL G		**G**	= £_______

STEP 4: Make the following deductions

		H	**£**_______
Deduct	(box 11.13)		– £_______
TOTAL I		**I**	= **£**_______

STEP 5: Now work out your savings and investment income

Add up the right hand boxes on page 3 of your Tax Return
(boxes 10.1, 10.4, 10.7, 10.8, 10.11, 10.14, 10.17, 10.20, 10.23, 10.26, 10.29, 10.32)
and write the total here **J** £ _______

The reason why savings and investment income is treated separately is that it is taxed at a lower rate of 20 per cent. Only higher-rate taxpayers need pay any extra tax. Those who pay basic rate tax of 23 per cent need not pay any more tax.

Now add I and J together   I + J = K   K   £_______

STEP 6: Now deduct what are known as charges

		K	£_______
Charitable covenants and gift aid	(add boxes 15.9 and 15.10 and multiply the figure by 100/77) (Note: if you are a non or lower taxpayer, the Inland Revenue may ask for the tax relief back.)		= £_______
TOTAL (known as Statutory Total Income)		**STI**	= £_______

STEP 7: Now deduct your personal allowances

Personal allowance either	£4045	
or if over 65 during tax year	£5220	
or if over 75 during tax year	£5400	
+ Blind person's allowance	£1280	
		– £_______

Note: Do not deduct the married couple's allowance at this stage.

If you are over 65 see the earnings rules in Chapter 9 on allowances in Part 2 of this book. You will need to do a separate calculation if your statutory total income (STI) is £15,600 or more in the tax year.

TOTAL (known as Taxable Income)   **TI**   = £_______

STEP 8: Now work out how much of your income falls into each tax band

Savings and investment income is calculated separately

Take your Taxable Income (TI) and deduct your savings and investment income (J)   **£**_______

Then multiply: the first £4100 by 20% = £_______
the next £22,000 by 23% = £_______
If you have any excess above £26,100:
multiply this by 40% **TAX 1** = **£**_______

If you have **any** income in the 40 per cent tax box in **TAX 1** you **will** have to pay extra tax on all your savings, investment and trust income – the total figure for **J**.

If this is the case, multiply **J** by 40% **TAX 2** = **£**_______

If you **do** not have any income in the 40 per cent tax box above you will have to calculate if you need to pay extra tax on your savings income.

If your Taxable Income (TI) **is less** than £26,100 you **will not** have to pay any extra tax on your savings, investment and trust income – the total figure for **J**.

If this is the case, multiply **J** by 20% **TAX 3** = **£**_______

If you do not have any income in the 40 per cent tax box above but your Taxable Income (TI) is more than £26,100, some of your savings and investment will be taxed at 20 per cent and some at 40 per cent. To find out how much is taxed at each rate do the following calculation.

Take your Taxable Income (TI) and deduct
your savings income (J) and then deduct
this figure from £26,100.
So £26,100 – (TI – J) = savings income
taxed at 20% **TAX 4** **£**_______
Now deduct £26,100 from TI:
TI – £26,100 = savings income taxed
at 40% **TAX 5** £_______

STEP 9: Work out your tax liability

Add any figures in TAX 1, 2, 3, 4 and 5 together £_______

Deduct your tax allowances that act as tax reducers. These are 15 per cent of:

married couple's allowance
additional personal allowance

widow's bereavement allowance
maintenance payments (under the £1830 rules) from box 15.4 or 15.5*

– £______

Fill £274.50 in the box for each one of these allowances (reduce the married couple's allowance if not for complete year)

Note: Special rules for over 65s and over 75s mean you will either have to enter 15 per cent of £3185 = £478 or 15 per cent of £3225 = £484. But remember, if your statutory total income (STI) is above £15,600 this allowance may be reduced.

This gives you the tax borne = £______

Add tax already deducted from things like charitable covenants and Gift Aid donations. Take the gross amount you gave (the donation x 100/77) and divide by 23 per cent. Put this figure in the box.

\+ £______

Add any tax relief you have been given on pension contributions. Again take the gross amount you paid in (your annual contributions x 100/77) and divide by 23 per cent. Put this figure in the box.

\+ £______

Total these up to give your tax liability **Tax liability** + £______

STEP 10: Now deduct any tax paid

Deduct taxes deducted at source from:

investment income in boxes 10.3, 10.6, 10.10, 10.13, 10.16, 10.19. 10.22, 10.25, 10.28 and 10.31 Total £______
your earnings from employment in box 1.11 £______
benefits and pensions in boxes 11.8 and 11.1
Other income in box 13.2 £______

* Note: if you have a figure in box 15.6 this qualifies for tax relief at your highest rate of tax. Now you know if you are a higher-rate taxpayer and if you can deduct this from your tax liability. Multiply the figure in box 15.6 by your highest rate of tax and then deduct that figure.

Deduct **tax paid** from your **tax liability** to calculate if you need to pay any extra tax – and how much – or if you are due a tax rebate. You will be owed a tax rebate if the tax already paid is greater than your tax liability.

Note: This calculation does not include all the possible figures, just the ones that are most likely to affect you.

You can now use this calculation to check the calculation you have done using the Inland Revenue Tax Calculation Guide. If the two figures are roughly the same you have probably not made an error.

If the two figures are widely different, check through your Tax Calculation Guide to make sure you have not made an error.

INDEX

capital gains tax 33–4, 174–82
  assets exempt 175–6
  assets liable to 175
  and your home 33, 179–80
charitable payments 78–9
children 44, 90–92
company cars 112–17

deadlines 4

employment 27–30, 95–129
  tax free employee benefits 104–6
employee expenses 118–20
  allowable expenses 125–8
employee share schemes 133–8

foreign income 32–3, 164–9
foreign pensions and benefits 167
foreign savings 166
freelance earnings 140
friendly societies 53
  death benefits 79–80

Gift Aid 78–9

income tax
  bands 13
  rates 13
Inland Revenue
  checks 9
  fines 4
interest-bearing securities 57

land and property 32, 157–63
  furnished holiday lettings
    159–60
  overseas lettings 167–8
life insurance policies 52–4
losses 58–60

maintenance
  received 49–52
  paid 74–7
married couples 42, 84–9
  and capital gains 180–81
mileage allowance 190–11
mortgages, MIRAS 71–3

National Insurance, for self-
    employed 152–4
National Savings 12
non-residence 34–5, 183–6
notional tax 55

offshore funds 168

partnerships 32, 155–6
pensions
  additional voluntary contributions
    55, 69
  received 45–9
  contributions 62–9
pensioners 15–16, 82, 86–7, 92–3
permanent health insurance 57
personal equity plans 37, 43

record keeping 6
redundancy 121–4
rent-a-room scheme 32, 158

savings and bank interest 36–40
  gross interest 37
  joint accounts 37
  offshore accounts 43
  tax free savings 37
SAYE schemes 134, 136
self-employment 31–2, 139–54
  allowable expenses 144–6
  capital allowances 149–52
share dividends 36–42
share options 30–31
social security benefits 12, 45–7
  taxable 46

tax allowances 14, 17, 81–94
tax calculations, doing it yourself 189
tax codes 16–20
tax collection 192
tax-free income 11
tax-free savings 37
tax-free investments 37
tax payments 4
tax relief 20–21, 61–80
tax repayments 190
tax return
  mistakes 8
  provisional figures 192
  the questionnaire 27–35
TESSAs 37, 43
trade union benefits 79–80
trusts 33, 170–73
  accumulation 171
  discretionary 171

unit trusts 37, 41–3

venture capital trusts 77
vocational training 70–71

working from home 146